GUIDE TO THE
MAMMALS
OF BRITAIN AND EUROPE

MAURICE BURTON

GUIDE TO THE
MAMMALS
OF BRITAIN AND EUROPE

illustrated by Rob van Assen, with
additional illustrations by Bryon Harvey
and Tony Morris; text on the habitats
of Europe by Christopher Barnard

ELSEVIER PHAIDON

© 1976 Elsevier Publishing Projects S.A., Lausanne

Produced by Elsevier International Projects Ltd., Oxford

Published by Elsevier Phaidon — an imprint of Phaidon Press Ltd.,
Littlegate House, St Ebbe's Street, Oxford.
ISBN: board edition 0 7290 0026 5
        paper edition 0 7290 0027 3
Filmset by Keyspools Limited, Golborne, Lancs

CONTENTS

PREFACE

This book has been designed and written with two ends in view. It describes not only the species of mammals found in Europe today, but also the different habitats that they occupy.

One should, however, beware of considering 'the mammals of Europe' as something stable. Climatic conditions have fluctuated since the last Ice Age and will continue to do so. As a result, mammalian populations will change as well. Not all mammals found in Europe today originated there, and new species are continually being introduced. If the populations of Europe as a whole are in a state of flux, the populations found in any particular habitat are even more liable to change. It is difficult to define a habitat with precision, and different habitats merge with one another and gradually change. Finally, mammals, being extremely adaptable, are rarely limited to a single habitat.

It follows, therefore, that in the introductory section of the book changes in the mammalian fauna of Europe since the Ice Age should be described, as are the changes in its zones of vegetation, for it is only by knowing the history of the region that the present mammalian distribution can be understood. The biological features of mammals that make them so adaptable are then discussed together with those characteristics, such as dentition, that aid their classification.

The main part of the book is composed of a comprehensive guide to every mammal species found in Europe, together with a discussion of their range, habits and life-history. They are arranged by habitat and each section is prefaced by a description of the habitat, the interrelationship of mammals within it, and the available foodstuffs which are so important a factor in the life of mammals. As has just been mentioned, mammals are adaptable and rarely limited exclusively to a single habitat. For this reason a feature of the book is a table which gives the range of alternative habitats in which each mammalian species may be seen.

INTRODUCTION

Europe today is vastly different from when Paleolithic man or his even earlier ancestors first set foot on it. Except in small patches the original vegetation is gone, even the soil has largely been transformed, and the original fauna has been altered either by the extinction of species, by their having adapted to changed conditions, or by the introduction of new species.

To say this is to state the obvious. Changes in climate have occurred, natural catastrophes have added their weight, but above all man, first by his hunting, then by his agriculture and his industrialization, has completely revolutionized the face of the land. All this is reflected in the mammalian fauna of Europe today.

The earliest mammals known, from anywhere in the world, were shrew-like. Their fossils have been found in the British Isles as well as in Africa and the Far East and they indicate that mammals first made their appearance 200 million years ago. This is 130 million years before the sudden and, to date, inexplicable demise of the dinosaurs, for whose extinction mammals have sometimes been blamed, almost certainly falsely.

Prior to the Industrial Revolution, still only two centuries ago, the biggest single event influencing the pattern of Europe's mammals, as seen today, was the period of the Ice Ages during which the polar ice cap spread south and again retreated four times. This period began about 600,000 years ago and ended about 15,000 years ago, the ice cap reaching as far south as 52–50 degrees latitude, so that at the height of the Ice Age half Europe was buried under glaciers. Even the southern, less frigid half, would have experienced temperatures far below those enjoyed today.

It is usual to say that "the plants and animals retreated before the advancing ice sheet". In doing so we put ourselves under the thrall of the tyranny of words. Expressed thus, the course of events is ridiculously over-simplified. For one thing, the southwards spread of the ice, and its corresponding withdrawal northwards, was ineffably slow. Plants do not move, in the sense of locomotion. The warmth-loving plants would die off first as the cold affected them but their seeds, carried southwards, finding equable conditions, would survive. The same sequence would probably obtain for all animals, including also the mammals, rather than an actual migratory movement to escape the slowly advancing cold conditions.

In fact, simple arithmetic shows that the advance and withdrawal of arctic conditions was, on average, at the rate of 1·6 km (1 mi) in 10,000 years. To a contemporary observer the resulting changes in the distribution of animals would have been less apparent than some taking place today. Nevertheless, the consequences can be exemplified by the cave paintings of reindeer in southwest Europe, hundreds of miles south of the nearest reindeer living today. As the final withdrawal of the ice cap took place, species established themselves in the relinquished areas from two directions: from northern Africa, and from Asia.

The upshot of the changes wrought by the Ice Ages was that a large area of land, now called Europe, was left covered by forest: mainly pines with birch in the north, deciduous forest in the middle belt and evergreen in the south, along the northern border of the Mediterranean. The continuous sheet of forest would be broken by large lakes and rivers as well as extensive marshes, like the Pripet Marshes, the result of water left behind by melting ice.

Basically, therefore, Europe's mammals, apart from aquatic species, bats and those few species that have found refuge on mountain tops, are forest dwellers. This is, however, another over-simplification. Forest is not easily defined: it may be dense or open, and both types thin out at the margins to areas of scattered trees and low scrub down to the water's edge, whether of lake, river or marsh. Just as there are gradations between forest and open grassland, dry areas and wet, lowland and highland, so the habitats of mammals cannot be clearly demarcated.

In Britain the Red deer lives on moors, but that is because the forests it used

A reconstruction of *Morganucodon*, the mammal that lived about 200 million years ago, which could be the ancestor to all mammals living today.

to inhabit have disappeared, their trees having been felled for industrial purposes. Our domestic cattle are kept in pastures but their ancestor, the Aurochs, lived in forests. Pigs are kept on farms but their ancestor was a forest dweller, as witness the fact that even domestic pigs, where given the opportunity, feed heavily on acorns in autumn.

Even forest dwellers can prefer open clearings for feeding, and this is exemplified by the Roe deer, that will forage today over fields but retire to woodlands to cud and to rest.

Although reduced in size today, the ice cap has never withdrawn entirely from Europe. Its fringes are present on the extreme north of the Scandinavian peninsula and the northern coast of European Russia. This is the tundra, the treeless zone, where the ground is perpetually cold and where conditions are found similar to those that prevailed at the edge of the ice cap as it fluctuated north and south across Europe over a period of half a million years. The southern boundary of the present-day tundra does not coincide with the Arctic Circle as delineated on the map of Europe, which is farther south, but with the mean isotherm of 10°C (50°F). The regions just south of this isotherm are denominated the subarctic which includes the taiga.

In Europe the tundra includes only the extreme northern fringes of Norway and Sweden, part of the Kola Peninsula and slightly more extensive tracts of northern European Russia. Its vegetation is sparse, mainly lichens and mosses with dwarf trees. Mammals are not much in evidence, except for the seals on the coastline. The Polar bear used to be seen there but human persecution has virtually eradicated it. There are also a few Wolves and the Arctic fox.

South of the tundra, and strictly part of subarctic Europe, is the region of the taiga or forest tundra, with belts of pine, fir, spruce and larch, interspersed with numerous lakes and marshes on the lowlands, as in Finland, with birch, aspen and willow supplementing the coniferous forests. Typical mammals are the Red squirrels and, on the ground, Reindeer and Elk, with Beavers in the marshes. Preying upon these are the Marten and Sable, Lynx and Wolverine, with Wolf and Bear as super-predators.

The taiga includes much of Scandinavia, almost all of Finland and the Soviet Union as far south as Leningrad, and somewhat farther south along a line from that city to the Urals.

Much of subarctic Europe is bare rock and where there is soil the climate, with its short summers, makes anything but the hardiest crops and the ubiquitous potato impossible to grow. The human populations are therefore sparse, their concentrations being south of the southern boundary of the subarctic. The area so occupied can be divided approximately into three regions: Continental, Atlantic and Mediterranean. The Continental region comprises most of European Russia, an area as large as the rest of Europe, a vast plain broken only by the Central Russian Uplands in the Moscow region, and by the Volga Heights. It is a region of relatively short summers and bitterly cold winters with most of the rain falling in summer. Being so far east it receives no benefit from the warm air associated with the North Atlantic Drift or Gulf Stream. This is felt by the second of the three regions, called for convenience the Atlantic region, where the winters are relatively mild and rain falls all the year round. It includes what is referred to politically as western

Europe, except that the Iberian peninsula and Italy are excluded. It also includes central Europe although this, to some extent, forms a transitional zone between the Atlantic and Continental regions.

The third of the subarctic regions, and therefore the fourth into which Europe can be divided climatically, is the Mediterranean region, including much of the Balkans. It is separated from the Atlantic region by a line of mountain ranges, from the Cantabrian Mountains and Pyrenees, through the Swiss Alps to the Transylvanian Alps. The line is much broken, and complicated especially at the eastern end by the Dinaric Alps of Yugoslavia, so that the northern boundary of the Mediterranean region is even more vague and diffuse than that drawn between the Atlantic and the Continental regions.

Europe Since the Ice Ages

Mammals, as we have seen, came into being just over 200 million years ago, at the start of the Mesozoic Era, the earliest mammal fossils discovered to date being of small, shrew-like animals. As time passed their descendants proliferated and diversified into distinct groups of small, medium-sized and large animals that spread throughout most of the world. Some fed solely on vegetation, others preyed upon these, and others, the omnivores, ate plant

Megaloceros, the Irish elk, a giant deer that lived in Europe during the Pleistocene. Its antlers were larger than those of any deer living today.

11

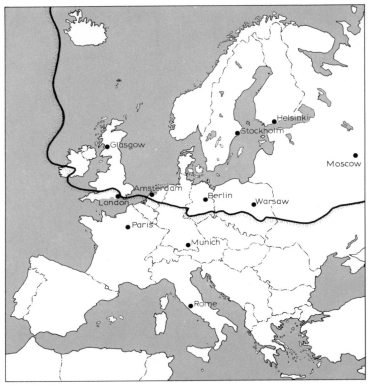

The maximum extent of the ice sheets during the last Ice Age. The main effect of this incursion was to make only the southern part of Europe available to mammals.

and animal food more or less indiscriminately. The evolution of some groups took place partly in Europe, but others evolved in Asia, Africa and elsewhere.

The changes were the result of genetic evolution, but affecting these tremendously have been two other major factors. One was the succession of Ice Ages, alternating with warm interglacial periods. During each Ice Age animals and plants underwent considerable changes of distribution. Evidence for this is seen in the cave drawings, already referred to, left by prehistoric man. The details of many distribution changes, however, can only be the subject of speculation aided by such evidence as can be dug out of the earth, supplemented by extrapolation from what can be gleaned from study of the living animals.

When the ice sheets extended southwards the extreme south of Europe, as well as North Africa and southwest Asia, formed a refuge for many species from which, during each interglacial, there was a two- or three-pronged invasion northwards.

During this same time man also settled in Europe, although the time and the means of his doing so are largely a matter of tenuous, if intelligent, speculation. We can be reasonably certain that the first settlements were of man the hunter, to be followed by man the tiller of the soil. The first persecuted the mammals direct, the latter burned the forests to till the soil. Their descendants did both and with acceleration as human populations grew apace, and especially as human society became industrialized. The total harassing of the mammalian fauna was accentuated by natural invasions of species, the House mouse and the Black and Brown rats are outstanding examples, and by man's habit of introducing species from other parts of the world, either for sport, for profit or solely from whim, or even fortuitously. It is almost certain, or at least strongly suspected, that some of the smaller rodents, indigenous to the mainland, were transported to islands off the coasts in bales of fodder carried in primitive boats by early man. The presence of the Common field mouse in Iceland is almost certainly the result of introduction by shipping. Even the spread of the House mouse and the two rats, from their original homes in central Asia, was probably aided by human food stores along the route. One consequence of all this is that, leaving aside the bats, which make up in numbers of species a high proportion of Europe's mammals, there is today a fair number of exotic mammals that have become feral in Europe. They compete with the native species for food and living space and present yet another changed circumstance to which the indigenous species must adapt.

The Habitats of Europe

It is usual in guides such as this one to arrange species in systematic order. That is to say, in the order in which they are classified. To that extent, this book is a break with tradition: a new arrangement has been adopted that is hoped will have a greater practical value. The systematic method dates from the early days of zoology, from the 16th century, and was the only reasonable way of listing the animals of a given region. The study of ecology, in which an organism is related to its environment or habitat, has burgeoned in the mid-20th century. It is therefore consistent with a modern view of biology that a field guide should be based on habitat. One value to the user is that it is possible, when in a wood, for instance, to be able to see at a glance what mammals may conceivably be present. To some extent this is an over-simplification because a wood in France, say, may contain one or more mammals that will be lacking in a wood in Yugoslavia. This drawback is, however, offset, since by arranging the mammals in small habitat groupings, the geographical distribution of the species within the Continent itself can be readily appreciated.

Even although the habitat method of grouping species can be justified on a priori grounds, it cannot be denied that there are inherent difficulties. First, habitats are not sharply circumscribed. Woodland may be a copse, wood or forest, it may include only coniferous trees or broadleaved trees, or a mixture

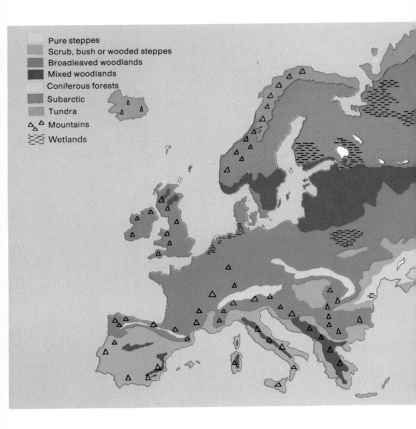

Pure steppes
Scrub, bush or wooded steppes
Broadleaved woodlands
Mixed woodlands
Coniferous forests
Subarctic
Tundra
△△ Mountains
Wetlands

The vegetation zones of Europe. These closely approximate to climatic zones and are the basis of the habitats as defined in this book. Zones are broadly indicated: local variation occurs where agricultural or urban development has been an important factor, and where there are major topographical features.

of the two. The second of these are often referred to as deciduous woodlands, but at least one conifer, the larch, is deciduous, and large numbers of others are evergreen.

Secondly, woodlands are a climax vegetation so we see all intermediates between them and grasslands with scrub and occasional trees that, under natural conditions, would revert to woodland proper.

Thirdly, mammals being so adaptable can usually thrive in habitats markedly different from the one in which they evolved. The Red squirrel, for example, is typically an inhabitant of pine forests. It can, nevertheless, adapt readily to broadleaved woods or parkland.

14

What are Mammals?

Mammals are a class of vertebrates, the Mammalia, distinguished by the possession of mammary glands in the female and in having hair on the body. Adult whales may appear completely hairless but have, in fact, a few bristles on the lips when young. Mammals are the most familiar animals mainly because they include domestic animals. Because so many are of large size they assume an importance out of proportion to their numbers, as well as playing a dominant role in the ecology of any area in which they are present. Indeed, while the biologist equates the name 'animal' with any living organism that is not plant, in popular usage it is often incorrectly regarded as being synonymous with mammals.

Of the 4,000 living mammalian species, rodents account for 1,500 and bats for a further 1,000. This total number compares with double the number of species of birds and well over 20,000 species of fishes. Moreover, only in a

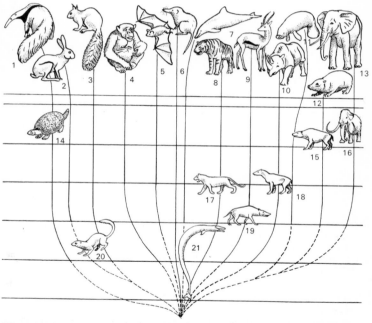

The evolution of the mammals. From origins during the Triassic period, 200 million years ago, diverse orders have evolved, the most important of which are indicated here. Representatives of each order are: (1) Anteater, (2) Hare, (3) Squirrel, (4) Chimpanzee, (5) Bat, (6) Shrew, (7) Dolphin, (8) Tiger, (9) Antelope, (10) Rhinoceros, (11) Sea-cow, (12) Hyrax, (13) Elephant, and fossil forms (14) Glyptodon, (15) Toxodon, (16) Mammoth, (17) Hoplophorus, (18) Moropus, (19) Bothriodon, (20) Paramys and (21) Zeuglodon.

few species of rodents do the world populations reach anything like the astronomical figures seen in many of the million species of insects. And although rodents are the most numerous of all mammals, only in a few species do the total populations reach hundreds of millions.

The range in size within the class Mammalia is enormous. The smallest species is usually quoted as Savi's pygmy or Etruscan shrew *Suncus etruscus* of Mediterranean Europe. It is 52mm (2in) long of which half is tail and it weighs 1·5–2gm ($\frac{1}{16}$oz) or less. The Palestine pygmy shrew *Crocidura religiosa* is, however, slightly smaller. The largest mammal, and the largest animal of all time, is the Blue whale *Balaenoptera musculus*. Before it was brought to the verge of extinction, by which time all large individuals had been slain, records of 30m (100ft) length or more and weights of 100 tons had been recorded, whilst some authors have even made claims of 36m (120ft) length and 170 tons weight.

The biological success of the mammals is owed in large measure to their homoiothermy (warm-bloodedness) which they share with the class Aves (birds). In reptiles, amphibians and fishes the body temperature varies with that of the environment. In mammals it is maintained at a fairly constant level of around 36°C (98°F). The coating of body hair acts as an insulator, preventing loss of heat in cold situations. In hot weather, however, excess heat is lost to the surrounding air by evaporation from sweat glands, another feature unique to mammals, or by panting. This temperature control enables mammals to live permanently at high altitudes, pikas at 3,353m (11,000ft) on Mt Everest, for example, and to exploit polar regions.

Even though able to regulate their temperature, small mammals tend to suffer from what has been called cold starvation. Small mammals have a greater surface area, in relation to their volume, than do large mammals. They are therefore more likely to lose body heat by radiation. This necessitates a proportionately greater need for food to replace the energy lost by this radiation. Small mammals, such as shrews, die of starvation if they go without food for more than two hours. Thus, small mammals that do not live underground or in the shelter of leaf litter or tall grass are vulnerable to low temperatures. They are thus particularly vulnerable during the winter and, as a result, have often solved their problems by hibernating.

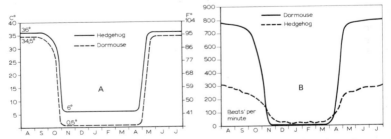

Hibernation involves profound physiological changes during the winter months. The body temperature is lowered (A) and the heart beat slowed down (B). Both changes enable food reserves of the body to be conserved.

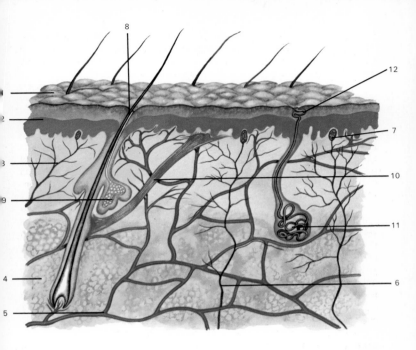

A section through mammalian skin showing the important anatomical features. The outer layer or epidermis is composed of two layers, the stratum corneum (1) and the statum granulosum or pigmented layer (2). Below this is the dermis (3) and the subcuticle layer (4). Organs contained within these layers are blood vessels (5), nerves (6), sense organs (7), hairs (8), sebaceous or oil glands (9), hair muscles (10), and sweat glands (11) that open on the surface through pores (12).

True hibernation is preceded by changes which alter the chemistry of the body in certain particulars. Then, when the ambient temperature falls to a critical point the hibernants retire to a prepared nest and fall into a deep sleep in which breathing is barely perceptible and the rate of heart beat falls to a very low figure. The precise time when hibernation begins is somewhat variable, thus, of three Hedgehogs from the same litter and living in captivity, under the same conditions, two fell into their winter sleep in mid-October and the third remained active for another two weeks. October is the normal time for hibernation of Hedgehogs to begin but it is by no means unknown for young individuals to remain active until the end of the year.

Hibernation differs in many ways from the winter torpor of reptiles and amphibians and the winter dormancy of bears, both of which are often referred to as hibernation. While in hibernation an animal relinquishes its temperature control' and becomes for the time being poikilothermic (cold-blooded).

17

The homoiothermy of mammals, the efficient metabolism resulting from it and thereby the adaptability of these animals in general, is linked with a number of anatomical features. The thoracic cavity is protected by a bony cage in which the ribs are joined to the breastbone by cartilage. A stout muscular sheet, the diaphragm, increases the strength and regularity of the breathing, so increasing the general efficiency of the metabolism. The heart is four-chambered, giving a double circulation with maximum metabolic efficiency. The aorta, the large blood vessel from the heart, has two arches in all reptiles except crocodiles. In birds and crocodiles the left arch has been lost, in mammals the right has been suppressed. The red blood cells in mammals lose their nuclei early in development, which increases their oxygen-carrying capacity leading to a constant high level of bodily activity.

Comparisons with birds and reptiles are necessary because the first of these are the only other homoiothermic class of animals and both they and mammals evolved from reptilian ancestors. One important feature of mammalian anatomy is the large brain, although in some mammals, namely the egg-laying monotremes of Australia, it is no larger nor more highly organized than the brain of reptiles. The larger, more highly organized brain of most mammals provides the intellectual versatility enabling a full exploitation of the opportunities opened up by homoiothermy especially in making use of a wider range of habitats and environments.

Some of the other distinguishing features of mammals include the small number of cervical vertebrae, a constant seven, except in manatees and sloths, whereas in reptiles and birds the number is much greater. The skull has two occipital condyles, the knobs of bone which articulate with the top of

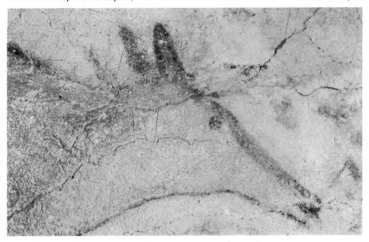

A painting from Altamira, typical of many that depict bison, deer, Wild boar and other mammals. Such paintings constitute some of the best evidence for the existence and distribution of post-Ice Age elements of the mammalian fauna.

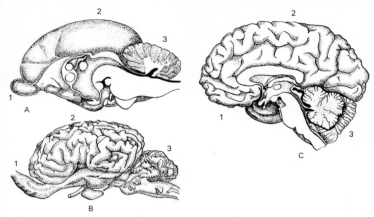

A comparison between sections through the brain of a primitive mammal, the Platypus (A), a Horse (B) and Man (C). The olfactory lobe (1) becomes smaller indicating lessening reliance on smell; the cerebrum, the centre of co-ordination (2) becomes increasingly convoluted; and the cerebellum, also a centre of co-ordination (3), becomes relatively large especially in 'higher' mammals. The sections are not drawn to scale.

the backbone or vertebral column, whereas in reptiles there is only one condyle. The lower jaw is made up of one bone instead of several as in all other vertebrates. The teeth consist of a set of milk teeth later replaced by a single permanent set, whereas in the lower vertebrates they are being constantly replaced throughout life. Also, they are socketed and found only in the jaws, with none on the palate as in some reptiles. A bony palate separates the breathing from the food passages, so a mammal can hold food in the mouth longer without interfering with the breathing, again resulting in a more efficient metabolism. The nasal cavities contain scroll-like turbinal bones covered with an olfactory membrane, giving a larger mucous surface and a more acute sense of smell. Instead of a single bone in the middle ear, as in reptiles, there is a chain of small bones, providing a more discriminating sense of hearing.

The Adaptability of Mammals

Their behaviour and physiology are so refined that the mammals can survive a variety of conditions that could not be tolerated by a snake or a lizard. As a result, we find that very few mammalian species are restricted to one particular habitat. An exception is, for example, the Polar bear which is found only in the extreme north of Europe. This species is therefore described in the section dealing with the subarctic. The rabbit on the other hand is found in a variety of habitats and the page on which its description occurs belongs to the section devoted to its typical habitat.

19

It would seem a simple matter to deal with animals according to habitat. It can be done readily with a few kinds of animals and also, doubtless, with the faunas of some areas of the world. With European mammals human history has a powerful bearing on their present geographical and topographical distribution, and especially on their need to adapt. Thus, in Europe today there are probably, and at most, only vestiges of the virgin habitat. Even in remote areas, which look to be unaffected by human activities, the impact of civilization, and especially of industrialization, must have been felt if only to a slight degree. The nearest to virgin conditions are those found on the higher levels of mountains where animals are, through the rigours of climate, scarce. Elsewhere there may be truly virgin environment but at most it will be in patches. The habitat of the completely aquatic mammals, the whales and seals, has been at least as badly disturbed though as a result of different factors.

To appreciate the present-day mammals it is best to approach the subject historically, tracing their fate as man first settled on that area of the Old World now named, politically, the continent of Europe. It is, in fact, a junior part of a large land-mass which also includes Asia and Africa, which is not insignificant in any review of the comings and goings of animal species.

If nothing else, where mammals are concerned, the mere human presence induces a secretive way of life, causing in some species a more nocturnal way of life than would otherwise be the case. Broadly speaking, therefore, we are faced with a not inconsiderable area of land surface that has for centuries

Mammals are successful largely because they are so adaptable. Here, a Common or Brown rat *Rattus norvegicus* is seen biting its tail in an attempt to free itself from a trap, and feeding on carrion in spite of the fact that its normal diet is herbivorous.

been wholly artificial, in which the animal populations and species have had to adapt to unnatural circumstances.

An outstanding example is the Wolf which formerly ranged over the whole continent. It is still present in the Iberian peninsula, central France, Italy, Sicily, Scandinavia, the Balkans and eastern Europe, especially European Russia. This takes no account of the Wolf as a wanderer and at times Wolves travel long distances and appear in unexpected places. In many areas where it can be said to be present its survival is precarious, and whereas it formerly inhabited plains and open woodlands, it has now retreated into large forests or mountains or sought refuge in other places, such as marshes, that cannot be regarded as its natural habitat. This is the result of continued and long sustained human persecution. The one certain statement is that everywhere the Wolf is declining in numbers. In the USSR, for example, where the anti-wolf campaign was vigorous, 42,600 kills were recorded for 1946 and this figure dropped to 8,800 in 1963.

Perhaps the best illustration of the relative adaptability of mammals is to be found in the fauna of Iceland. This country, Arctic in location but warmed by the Gulf Stream, is 320km (200mi) from Greenland and 725km (450mi) from the coast of Europe. Aside from the 17 species of cetaceans occasionally sighted off its coasts it has only 13 species of mammals. Seven of these are pinnipedes (seals and walrus), of which only two are resident and actually breed there, the others being casual visitors: the remainder include two carnivores and four rodents. Possibly the Reindeer might be included but even this is doubtful. Three Reindeer were introduced in 1771 and 70 more during 1777–1787, but they competed with the sheep and were killed off except in the north-east of the country where a protected stock of upwards of 500 individuals may be found. During the 1920's and 1930's attempts were made to introduce the Musk-ox, Silver fox, Mink and several other fur-bearing mammals, such as the Rabbit and the Restless cavy, but these met with little success.

The two carnivores are the Polar bear and the Arctic fox. The first is a casual visitor reaching Iceland on ice floes. The fox is represented mainly by a variety or mutant called the Blue fox. The four rodents are the House mouse, Common field mouse, Black rat and Brown rat. All four have reached Iceland through human agency. The Brown rat is believed to have arrived at some time in the early eighteenth century. The first record for the Black rat is dated 1919. The two mice are believed to have been carried there in stores and bales of fodder transported by the first settlers in the 9th century.

The Field mouse was especially successful, not only invading houses in competition with the House mouse but spreading all over the country, even, it is said, crossing rivers. The method by which they are alleged to do this, according to J. Steenstrup, writing in 1868, is as follows: "Their boats are dry cowdung, such as is dropped upon the fields, namely thin and flat. So many as intend to travel in company, four to six or ten at the utmost, help each other to carry their boat to the water. The cargo is a considerable heap of *Arbutus* berries, which are piled up in the middle, but the mice sit in a circle outside them, so that their heads meet together in the middle point, but their tails hang out in the water, and are employed as oars in making the passage''.

Tracking Techniques

Excluding bats, most European mammals are difficult to observe. Some are strictly nocturnal or crepuscular and those that are active by day either move about under cover, or readily make for cover at the approach of a human observer. All, however, leave some trace of their activities, although some of these are difficult to see. Moreover, it requires skill born mainly of experience both to locate and interpret these traces. What follows here is therefore an attempt to indicate how this skill may be acquired.

Pathways and runs. Most terrestrial mammals keep to regular pathways in moving from a resting place to a feeding ground. Exceptions are the predators, like the fox, that range in an irregular manner in search of prey. Along these pathways the vegetation or the surface of the soil becomes flattened or tamped down, and does not necessarily bear traces of footprints. The width of the pathway gives some indication of the size of the animal. Where the pathway passes under tussocky grass or low branches some indication of the height of the animal can be obtained.

Some mammals tend to follow hedge bottoms or move along the base of a stone wall or along the bottom of an overgrown ditch where their pathways are difficult to follow. Water voles prefer the overhanging vegetation on the banks of streams to open ground. Where grass is long, Rabbits use tunnels through it, as mice, voles and shrews do through shorter grasses.

Another clue to the presence of mammals is the scratch marks on trees where an animal has climbed or sought to climb a trunk. The commonest are those of squirrels, which start 0·6m (2ft) up from the ground, where the animal has taken an upward leap. Lower and smaller versions are the work of dormice. Regular scratching places are often the work of Badgers and cats.

Moles make slightly zigzag surface runs, with the earth upheaved into a ridge and cracked along the top. Badgers sometimes open these up to produce a track that is difficult to interpret.

Tracks. Nothing more certainly identifies an animal than its footprints, but except to the experienced tracker there is nothing that can so readily bring disappointment. Only on firm mud can footprints be perfectly outlined. Hard ground will show only the tracks of large, heavy animals. Tracks on sand readily disintegrate as do those in snow. On wet ground, water seeps and blurs the outlines. Windblown dust, leaves and other debris tend to obliterate. Yet even these changes that tend to obscure can tell much, because they indicate the age of the prints.

Once the tracks have been identified other things can be deduced from them. Thus, the tracks of the older individuals are deeper and broader than average and the stride is longer. Male prints are larger than those of a female, except in rodents in which the female is larger than the male. Male footprints tend to be nearer the midline and are more direct in line because the female tends to swing her hips from side to side, while a pregnant female tends to straddle, and the later the pregnancy the deeper the tracks because of her added weight.

The speed at which an animal has travelled may be indicated by the lengthening or shortening of the stride. Tracks also vary according to whether

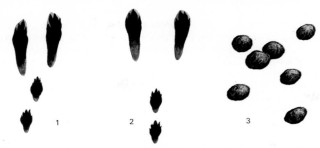

Signs of the presence of the Rabbit *Oryctolagus cuniculus*. (1) Tracks left when hopping, (2) when running and (3) droppings.

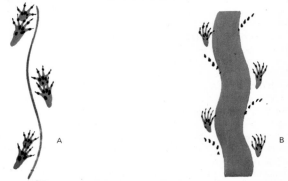

Tracks of the Common vole *Microtus arvalis* (A) in which the trail left by the tail separates right and left footprints, and the Mole *Talpa europaea* (B) in which there is a marked difference between fore and hind footprints and in which the body leaves a broad trail.

the animal has walked, trotted or galloped. Short steps and scuffled tracks are made by exhausted, sick or injured animals. And small footprints with a furrow between show that a rat has passed dragging its tail.

Burrows and other homes. Tracks and pathways often lead to a resting place, or home. Small to medium-sized mammals usually shelter in the ground, in a burrow called a set (Badger), earth (fox) or holt (Otter). Exceptions include Weasels, Stoats, polecats and martens. Burrows are typically tunnel formations and the diameter of the entrance gives a fair clue to the size of the tunneler because most animals make the entrance only sufficiently large for the body to pass through comfortably. Badgers make larger entrance holes than are necessary for their girth, but the presence of a Badger set is betrayed by a conspicuous threshold of excavated earth. Some mammals use larger holes, when they take over burrows formerly used by larger animals. A fox may use a Badger set or a rat may occupy a Rabbit burrow.

The smallest holes are made by shrews, barely 25mm (1in) in diameter.

Those of mice, Bank and Field voles are slightly larger. The burrow of a Brown rat is 75–100mm (3–4in) in diameter.

Spider webs over entrances to burrows show they are not now in use.

Tooth marks. Two types of tooth marks more especially indicate the kind of animal that has been at work, those made by rodents and carnivores. Rodent incisor teeth of upper and lower jaws leave unmistakable marks, the width of each tooth mark giving an indication of the size of the species responsible. Those of House mice and rats are familiar on woodwork of houses, on lead pipes and on bones. Archaeologists have sometimes found bones decorated as if by early man when they are no more than scored by the teeth of rats. Putty in window frames is sometimes nibbled by rodents, so are electric cables.

Tooth marks can also be seen on nutshells and on the remains of berries and seeds and these help to identify the feeder. The manner of opening a nut and the method of chewing wheat grains are both diagnostic. Fieldmice and dormice nibble the shell in different ways. Squirrels open hazel nuts by making a nick at the side of the apex then insert an incisor to split the shell lengthwise into equal halves.

Rats, the Bank vole and field mice eat cereal grains by starting at the germ end and then proceed to devour it lengthwise as a monkey would eat a banana. House mice nibble the grains at the middle rotating the grain as they gnaw.

The other group, the carnivores, sometimes bite rubber-covered flex or stout wire, leaving the marks of their carnassial teeth.

Other tell-tale signs. A Red fox often beheads the bird it kills, leaving the head behind.

Weasels and Stoats kill with a bite near the base of the skull.

Badgers eat small invertebrates and also larger prey such as ducks and poultry. They savage these larger prey and will lacerate the carcase of a deer.

Bunches of hair, sometimes left on brambles and barbed wire, help to identify animals that have passed by.

Mammal hair is greasy. Some mammals rub their flanks on trees or rocks leaving greasy marks. Such marks may sometimes be seen on the sides of a burrow. Rats regularly clambering among woodwork leave a conspicuous greasy smear.

Teeth in Classification and Identification

The most important character used in the identification of mammals is the dentition, the collective name of the teeth in both halves of the upper and lower jaws. To a large extent the subdivision of the Mammalia is based on differences in dentition. A typical mammalian dentition includes incisors, canines, premolars and molars. Some species lack one or more of these categories of teeth. Among European mammals, for example, the lagomorphs (rabbits and hares), the rodents and the Artiodactyla or cloven-hoofed animals, with few exceptions, lack canines.

Broadly speaking, the incisors are for seizing small prey (they may also be

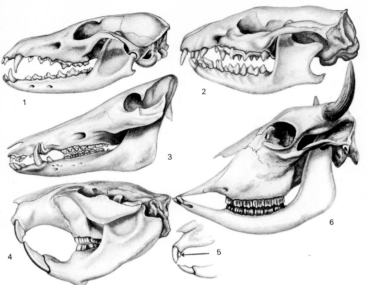

Teeth in various mammalian groups. (1) Carnivores have long canines, and molars and premolars modified as carnassials. (2) Insectivores have pointed cheek teeth. (3) Artiodactyls are characterized by low molar teeth that are used to grind vegetable food. (4) Rodents have chisel-shaped incisors for gnawing, and a marked diastema or gap between these and the cheek teeth. (5) Lagomorphs are similar to rodents but have second incisors lying behind the upper incisors. Finally, perissodactyls such as horses (6) have large molars for grinding, and a long diastema.

used for nibbling the fur in grooming), the canines are used for slashing blows during aggressive behaviour or for subduing and holding larger prey, and the premolars and molars (together known as the cheek teeth) for masticating.

The teeth are important indicators of both the diet and the method of feeding. The Insectivora, the most primitive of the true or placental mammals (Eutheria), which includes shrews, Hedgehogs, moles and desmans, have a dentition suited to seizing, holding and chewing insects. The most characteristic feature is the small cusps or points on the upper surface of the cheek teeth. The dentition of bats is similar to that of insectivores, and that of the primates, which include lemurs, monkeys, apes and man, is also similar although the crowns of the cheek teeth have more flattened and rounded cusps.

Rodents, often justifiably called gnawing animals, are typified by having prominent incisors, few in number, with chisel-shaped edges. These grow continuously at the roots and are kept in check by their owners constantly gritting their teeth and chewing, either food or inedible substances. Grey squirrels are notorious for chewing metal objects such as lead name labels on garden trees. Rodents lack canines and there is a wide gap, the diastema, between the incisors and the first cheek teeth into which the flesh of the lips can be drawn in order to block temporarily the passage to the mouth. So a squirrel, for example, can chew lead without swallowing the chips, which fall harmlessly from the front part of the mouth.

Rabbits and hares used to be classified as a subdivision of the order Rodentia, in the suborder Duplicidentata, differing from other rodents in having a second, much smaller, incisor behind each of the incisors of the upper jaw. There are other points of difference, in the skull and in anatomical and behavioural features, and it is agreed that the segregation of these animals in a separate order, the Lagomorpha, is justified.

The next order, the Carnivora or flesh-eaters, are characterized by the size of the canines, which form fangs, but above all by the presence of one pair of teeth on each side of the jaw, the last upper premolar and the first lower molar, which form carnassials, or flesh teeth, each with a sharp, ridge-like cusp, used in shearing flesh. In bears the cheek teeth have more flattened crowns, linked with their omnivorous diet, and so do hyaenas that crush large bones.

Seals, sealions and walruses were formerly included in the order Carnivora, in the suborder Pinnipedia. They have now been classified into a separate order, the Pinnipedia. Their cheek teeth are uniform and usually pointed and recurved, a form regarded as an adaptation for holding slippery prey, such as fish.

The Artiodactyla (cloven-hoofed animals) usually lack canines, in many there are incisors in the lower jaw only and the cheek teeth are uniform in shape and bear ridges on the crowns, for crushing and masticating fibrous plant food.

The order Cetacea (whales, dolphins and porpoises) is classified into two suborders, the Mysticeti or Whalebone whales, which lack teeth, and the Odontoceti or Toothed whales typically with numerous peg-like teeth, more or less uniform in size and shape, and without distinction into incisors, canines and cheek teeth. These also appear to be an adaptation for holding slippery prey.

Where the teeth are clearly divided into incisors, canines, premolars and molars it is usual to express their number and position in a dental formula, thus: i $\frac{3}{3}$, c $\frac{1}{1}$, pm $\frac{4}{4}$, m $\frac{2}{3}$ or, more simply, $\frac{3142}{3143}$. This formula indicates the presence of three incisors in each half of both upper and lower jaws, a single canine in each half of each jaw, four premolars in each half of each jaw, two molars in each half of the upper jaw and three in each half of the lower jaw. The dental formula is usually constant for a species but there are difficulties with the voles because in them there may be variation within a species and there is sometimes doubt whether a particular tooth is the last premolar or the first molar. Shrews also present a problem, having no canines or several. In what follows the generally accepted formula is used for all these. Similar doubts are found in some of the Artiodactyla, and here also an arbitrary decision has to be taken.

Dental Formulae

INSECTIVORA

Erinaceus	$\frac{3\ 1\ 3\ 3}{2\ 1\ 2\ 3}$
Sorex	$\frac{1\ 5\ 1\ 3}{1\ 1\ 1\ 3}$
Neomys, Suncus	$\frac{1\ 4\ 1\ 3}{1\ 1\ 1\ 3}$
Crocidura	$\frac{1\ 3\ 1\ 3}{1\ 1\ 1\ 3}$
Desmana, Galemys, Talpa	$\frac{3\ 1\ 4\ 3}{3\ 1\ 4\ 3}$

CHIROPTERA

Nycteris, Vespertilio	$\frac{2\ 1\ 1\ 3}{3\ 1\ 2\ 3}$
Rhinolophus	$\frac{1\ 1\ 2\ 3}{2\ 1\ 3\ 3}$
Myotis	$\frac{2\ 1\ 3\ 3}{3\ 1\ 3\ 3}$
Miniopterus, Plecotus	$\frac{2\ 1\ 2\ 3}{3\ 1\ 3\ 3}$
Barbastella, Nyctalus, Pipistrellus	$\frac{2\ 1\ 2\ 3}{3\ 1\ 2\ 3}$
Lasiurus, Tadarida	$\frac{1\ 1\ 2\ 3}{3\ 1\ 2\ 3}$

PRIMATES

Macaca	$\frac{2\ 1\ 2\ 3}{2\ 1\ 2\ 3}$

LAGOMORPHA

Lepus, Oryctolagus	$\frac{1(1)\ 0\ 3\ 3}{1\ \ \ 0\ 2\ 3}$

RODENTIA

Citellus, Marmota, Pteromys, Sciurus	$\frac{1\ 0\ 2\ 3}{1\ 0\ 1\ 3}$
Castor, Dryomys, Eliomys, Glis, Hystrix, Muscardinus, Myocastor, Myominus	$\frac{1\ 0\ 1\ 3}{1\ 0\ 1\ 3}$
Acomys, Apodemus, Arvicola, Clethrionomys, Cricetulus, Cricetus, Dicrostonyx, Dolomys, Lemmus, Mesocricetus, Micromys, Microtus, Myopus, Mus, Ondatra, Pitymys, Rattus, Spalax	$\frac{1\ 0\ 0\ 3}{1\ 0\ 0\ 3}$
Sicista	$\frac{1\ 0\ 1\ 3}{1\ 0\ 0\ 3}$

CARNIVORA

Alopex, Canis, Nyctereutes, Vulpes	$\frac{3\ 1\ 4\ 2}{3\ 1\ 4\ 3}$
Thalarctos, Ursus	$\frac{3\ 1\ 4\ 2\text{-}3}{3\ 1\ 4\ 2\text{-}3}$
Genetta, Herpestes, Procyon	$\frac{3\ 1\ 4\ 2}{3\ 1\ 4\ 2}$
Meles $\quad\frac{3\ 1\ 3\ 1}{3\ 1\ 4\ 2}$ sometimes	$\frac{3\ 1\ 4\ 1}{3\ 1\ 4\ 2}$
Mustela, Putorius, Vormela	$\frac{3\ 1\ 3\ 1}{3\ 1\ 3\ 2}$
Lutra	$\frac{3\ 1\ 3\ 2}{3\ 1\ 3\ 2}$
Gulo, Martes	$\frac{3\ 1\ 4\ 1}{3\ 1\ 4\ 2}$
Felis	$\frac{3\ 1\ 3\ 1}{3\ 1\ 2\ 1}$
Lynx	$\frac{3\ 1\ 2\ 1}{3\ 1\ 2\ 1}$

ARTIODACTYLA

Sus	$\frac{3\ 1\ 4\ 3}{3\ 1\ 4\ 3}$
Cervus, Hydropotes, Muntiacus, Rangifer, Sika	$\frac{0\ 1\ 3\ 3}{4\ 0\ 3\ 3}$
Alces, Bison ; Capra, Capreolus, Dama, Odocoileus, Ovibos, Ovis, Rupicapra	$\frac{0\ 0\ 3\ 3}{4\ 0\ 3\ 3}$
Saiga	$\frac{0\ 0\ 3\ 3}{4\ 0\ 2\ 3}$

PINNIPEDIA

Odobenus	$\frac{3\ 1\ 3\ 2}{3\ 1\ 3\ 1}$
Erignathus, Halichoerus, Pagophilus, Phoca, Pusa	$\frac{3\ 1\ 4\ 1}{2\ 1\ 4\ 1}$
Cystophora	$\frac{2\ 1\ 4\ 1}{1\ 1\ 4\ 1}$
Monachus	$\frac{2\ 1\ 4\ 1}{2\ 1\ 4\ 1}$

Classification of the Mammals of the World

SUBCLASS PROTOTHERIA, the monotremes or egg-laying mammals, including the echidna (Spiny anteater) and the Duckbill or Platypus. Australia and adjacent islands.

SUBCLASS METATHERIA, the marsupials or pouched mammals, including such forms as kangaroos, opossums, phalangers, koalas. Australia and adjacent islands, South America and one species in North America.

SUBCLASS EUTHERIA, true or placental mammals divided into 18 orders:

Order Insectivora, hedgehogs, shrews, moles, tenrecs, desmans

Order Dermoptera, 'flying lemur'

Order Tupaioidea, tree shrews

Order Chiroptera, bats

Order Primates, lemurs, monkeys, apes, man

Order Edentata, anteaters, sloths, armadillos

Order Pholidota, pangolins

Order Lagomorpha, rabbits, hares, pikas or mouse-hares

Order Rodentia, squirrels, rats, mice, voles, porcupines

Order Carnivora, dogs, bears, raccoons, weasels, genets, mongooses, hyaenas, cats

Order Pinnipedia, seals

Order Tubulidentata, aardvark

Order Proboscidea, elephants

Order Hyracoidea, hyraxes or dassies

Order Sirenia, manatees, dugong

Order Perissodactyla, horses, asses, zebras, tapirs, rhinoceroses

Order Artiodactyla, pigs, hippopotamuses, camels, deer, giraffes, cattle, sheep, goats, antelopes

Order Cetacea, whales, dolphins, porpoises

European Species in Systematic Order

This table shows the distribution of mammals in Europe and their habitat preferences. Typical habitats are indicated by ●, other habitats where a species may occur by ●. The habitat under which a species is described in this guide is indicated in red.

	Distribution in Europe	Pure steppes	Scrub, bush or wooded steppes	Human habitations	Broadleaved woodlands	Mixed woodlands	Coniferous forests	Mountains	Wetlands	Subarctic	Erratics
Class Mammalia											
ORDER INSECTIVORA											
Family Erinaceidae											
European hedgehog *Erinaceus europaeus*	whole continent except for extreme north		●		●	●	●				
					fringes of woods mainly						
Algerian or Vagrant hedgehog *Erinaceus algirus*	coast of Mediterranean, France and Spain		●		●	●	●				
					fringes of woods mainly						
Family Soricidae											
Pygmy shrew *Sorex minutus*	whole continent except Iberia and Mediterranean islands		●								
Common shrew *Sorex araneus*	whole continent except Ireland, most of Iberia, and Mediterranean islands	●	●		●	●	●		●		
Masked or Laxman's shrew *Sorex caecutiens*	very localized and mainly in north of continent	●			●	●	●				●
Least shrew *Sorex minutissimus*	rare : central Finland, northern and central Russia		●				●				
Alpine shrew *Sorex alpinus*	central Europe							●	●		
European water shrew *Neomys fodiens*	whole continent except Ireland, most of Iberia and Balkans								●		
Mediterranean or Miller's water shrew *Neomys anomalus*	western and central Europe, Balkans								●	●	

29

	Distribution in Europe	Pure steppes	Scrub, bush or wooded steppes	Human habitations	Broadleaved woodlands	Mixed woodlands	Coniferous forests	Mountains	Wetlands	Subarctic	Erratics
Savi's pygmy or Etruscan shrew *Suncus etruscus*	Mediterranean Europe and southeast France		●	●							
Bicoloured white-toothed shrew *Crocidura leucodon*	central Europe mainly		●	●							
Lesser white-toothed or Scilly shrew *Crocidura suaveolens*	central and southern Europe; absent from most of Iberia		●	●	●	●	●				
					fringes of woods only						
Common European white-toothed shrew *Crocidura russula*	central and southern Europe	●	●	●	●	●	●				
					fringes of woods						

Family Talpidae

	Distribution in Europe	Pure steppes	Scrub, bush or wooded steppes	Human habitations	Broadleaved woodlands	Mixed woodlands	Coniferous forests	Mountains	Wetlands	Subarctic	Erratics
Pyrenean desman *Galemys pyrenaicus*	northern Iberia								●		
Russian desman *Desmana moschata*	southeastern Europe								●		
Common mole *Talpa europaea*	whole continent except most of Scandinavia, Ireland, western and southern Iberia, and Balkans	●	●	●	●	●	●	●	●		
Mediterranean or Blind mole *Talpa caeca*	Mediterranean region	●	●	●	●	●	●	●	●		
Roman mole *Talpa romana*	southern Italy, Sicily, Corfu, Greece	●	●	●	●	●	●	●	●		

ORDER CHIROPTERA

Family Nycteridae

	Distribution in Europe	Pure steppes	Scrub, bush or wooded steppes	Human habitations	Broadleaved woodlands	Mixed woodlands	Coniferous forests	Mountains	Wetlands	Subarctic	Erratics
Egyptian slit-faced or Hollow-faced bat *Nycteris thebaica*	Corfu only, as a rare vagrant										●

Family Rhinolophidae

	Distribution in Europe	Pure steppes	Scrub, bush or wooded steppes	Human habitations	Broadleaved woodlands	Mixed woodlands	Coniferous forests	Mountains	Wetlands	Subarctic	Erratics
Greater horseshoe bat *Rhinolophus ferrum-equinum*	southern and south-central Europe, southern England and Wales				●	●	●				

	Pure steppes	Scrub, bush or wooded steppes	Human habitations	Broadleaved woodlands	Mixed woodlands	Coniferous forests	Mountains	Wetlands	Subarctic	Erratics

Distribution in Europe

Species	Distribution in Europe	Pure steppes	Scrub, bush or wooded steppes	Human habitations	Broadleaved woodlands	Mixed woodlands	Coniferous forests	Mountains	Wetlands	Subarctic	Erratics
Lesser horseshoe bat *Rhinolophus hipposideros*	similar to preceding species but northern boundary of range slightly farther north				●	●	●				
Mediterranean horseshoe bat *Rhinolophus euryale*	Mediterranean				●	●	●				
Blasius' horseshoe bat *Rhinolophus blasii*	Balkans, Italy, Sicily				●	●	●				
Mehely's horseshoe bat *Rhinolophus mehelyi*	southern Europe, very localized				●	●	●				

Family Vespertilionidae

Species	Distribution in Europe	Pure steppes	Scrub, bush or wooded steppes	Human habitations	Broadleaved woodlands	Mixed woodlands	Coniferous forests	Mountains	Wetlands	Subarctic	Erratics
Daubenton's or Water bat *Myotis daubentoni*	whole continent except extreme north and south-east				●	●	●		●	●	
Long-fingered bat *Myotis capaccinii*	central Mediterranean north to Hungary				●	●	●		●	●	
Pond bat *Myotis dasycneme*	Low Countries eastwards to Russia				●	●	●		●	●	
Whiskered bat *Myotis mystacinus*	whole of continent except for extreme north and southern half of Iberia				●	●					
Ikonnikov's bat *Myotis ikonnikovi*	Sophia (Bulgaria) and Ruthenian Carpathians										●
Brandt's bat *Myotis brandtii*	central to western Europe										●
Geoffroy's bat *Myotis emarginatus*	central to southern Europe				●	●					
Natterer's bat *Myotis nattereri*	whole continent except most of Scandinavia and the Balkans			●	●	●					
Bechstein's bat *Myotis bechsteini*	discontinuous distribution in western, central and southern Europe				●	●					
Large mouse-eared bat *Myotis myotis*	central and southern Europe			●							

	Pure steppes	Scrub, bush or wooded steppes	Human habitations	Broadleaved woodlands	Mixed woodlands	Coniferous forests	Mountains	Wetlands	Subarctic	Erratics
Distribution in Europe										
Lesser mouse-eared bat — *Myotis oxygnathus* — southern Europe			●							
Long-eared bat — *Plecotus auritus* — whole continent except northern Scandinavia to northern Russia			●	●	●	●				
Grey long-eared bat — *Plecotus austriacus* — central and southern Europe	●	●	●	●	●					
Schreiber's bat — *Miniopterus schreibersi* — southern Europe	●	●								
Barbastelle — *Barbastella barbastellus* — western to central Europe (France to Poland), localized elsewhere				●	●	●	●	●		
Common pipistrelle — *Pipistrellus pipistrellus* — whole continent except in extreme north			●	●						
Nathusius' pipistrelle — *Pipistrellus nathusii* — eastern Europe, localized in western Europe				●	●	●	●			
Kuhl's pipistrelle — *Pipistrellus kuhli* — south-western Europe and Mediterranean			●							
Savi's pipistrelle — *Pipistrellus savii* — southern Europe							●			
Serotine — *Eptisecus serotinus* — all Europe south of Baltic, also southern England			●	●	●	●				
Northern bat — *Vespertilio nilssoni* — mainly northern, localized in central Europe							●		●	
Parti-coloured bat — *Vespertilio murinus* — mainly eastern Europe, localized elsewhere			●	●	●		●			
Common noctule — *Nyctalus noctula* — whole continent except extreme north, Scottish highlands, Ireland and northwest Iberia		●	●	●	●					
Lesser noctule or Leisler's bat — *Nyctalus leisleri* — cental and eastern Europe, local in western Europe				●	●	●				
Hoary bat — *Lasiurus cinereus* — N. American species found once in Iceland, once on Orkneys										●

Note (Nathusius' pipistrelle): fringes of woods only

32

	Distribution in Europe	Pure steppes	Scrub, bush or wooded steppes	Human habitations	Broadleaved woodlands	Mixed woodlands	Coniferous forests	Mountains	Wetlands	Subarctic	Erratics
Family Molossidae											
European free-tailed bat *Tadarida teniotis*	southern Europe, especially Mediterranean			●							
ORDER PRIMATES											
Family Cercopithecidae											
Barbary ape *Macaca sylvanus*	Gibraltar only: almost certainly introduced										●
ORDER LAGOMORPHA											
Family Leporidae											
Rabbit *Oryctolagus cuniculus*	southwest Europe originally but widely introduced elsewhere	●	●		●	●	●				
Mountain Varying or Blue hare *Lepus timidus*	northern Europe, Ireland, Scottish highlands, Swiss Alps				●	●		●			
Cape or Brown hare *Lepus capensis*	whole continent except Scandinavia to northern Russia and most of Ireland	●	●		●	●					
ORDER RODENTIA											
Family Sciuridae											
Red squirrel *Sciurus vulgaris*	whole continent except Mediterranean islands and much of England						●				
Grey squirrel *Sciurus carolinensis*	British Isles only: introduced			●	●	●	●				●
European suslik *Citellus citellus*	eastern Europe (East Germany to Bulgaria)	●						●			
Spotted suslik *Citellus suslicus*	eastern Europe, mainly southern Russia	●						●			
Marmot *Marmota marmota*	Swiss Alps mainly, local in Carpathians							●			
Russian flying squirrel *Pteromys volans*	Finland, northern Russia					●	●				

also birch woods

33

Family / Species	Distribution in Europe	Pure steppes	Scrub, bush or wooded steppes	Human habitations	Broadleaved woodlands	Mixed woodlands	Coniferous forests	Mountains	Wetlands	Subarctic	Erratics
Family Castoridae											
European beaver *Castor fiber*	formerly extensive, now localized and mainly in northern half; also in Rhône Valley								●		
Family Gliridae											
Garden or Oak dormouse *Eliomys quercinus*	central and southern Europe		●	●	●	●	●	●			
Forest dormouse *Dryomys nitedula*	eastern Europe, south to Greece				●	●	●				
Edible Fat or Squirrel-tailed dormouse *Glis glis*	central and southern Europe			●	●	●					
Common or Hazel dormouse *Muscardinus avellanarius*	similar to *Glis* but including southern half of Britain and southern Sweden				●	●	●				
Mouse-like or Ognev's dormouse *Myomimus personatus*	Asiatic species, Bulgaria only				●	●					●
Family Cricetidae											
Common hamster *Cricetus cricetus*	eastern central Europe	●	●								
Grey or Migratory hamster *Cricetulus migratorius*	southern Russia, localized in Bulgaria and Greece		●								
Golden hamster *Mesocricetus auratus*	Rumania and Bulgaria only	●	●								
Family Microtidae											
Arctic lemming *Dicrostonyx torquatus*										●	
Wood lemming *Myopus schisticolor*	Scandinavia, Finland, northern Russia						●				
Norway lemming *Lemmus lemmus*	Scandinavia only						●				
Ruddy or Northern red-backed vole *Clethrionomys rutilus*	extreme north									●	

	Pure steppes	Scrub, bush or wooded steppes	Human habitations	Broadleaved woodlands	Mixed woodlands	Coniferous forests	Mountains	Wetlands	Subarctic	Erratics
Distribution in Europe										
Common redbacked or Bank vole *Clethrionomys glareolus* — whole continent except extreme north, Ireland, Iberia, Italy, Greece		•		•	•	•				
Large-toothed red-backed or Grey-sided vole *Clethrionomys rufocanus* — Scandinavia mainly									•	
Nehring's snow vole *Dolomys milleri* — Yugoslavia only and there localized							•			
Water vole *Arvicola terrestris* — whole continent except southern Italy, Greece and Mediterranean islands								•		
European pine vole *Pitymys subterraneus* — central Europe, France to southern Russia		•	•	•	•	•	rarely	•		
Fatio's pine or Root vole *Pitymys incertus* — Alps only							•			
Savi's pine or Mediterranean root vole *Pitymys savii* — northern Iberia, southern France to Italy, Sicily; localized in Yugoslavia							•			
Mediterranean pine or Iberian root vole *Pitymys duodecimcostatus* — Iberia, southern France							•	•		
Common vole *Microtus arvalis* — whole continent except northern Europe, Iberia and most of Mediterranean, also Orkneys	•	•	•							
Field or Short-tailed vole *Microtus agrestis* — whole continent except Ireland and most of Mediterranean region as well as Rumania	•	•		•	•	•		•		
Root vole *Microtus ratticeps* — mainly eastern half of Europe, but mostly localized; also one small area in Holland								•		
Snow or Alpine vole *Microtus nivalis* — southern Europe							•			
Guenther's or Mediterranean vole *Microtus guentheri* — Balkans only	•	•	•				•			

35

	Pure steppes	Scrub, bush or wooded steppes	Human habitations	Broadleaved woodlands	Mixed woodlands	Coniferous forests	Mountains	Wetlands	Subarctic	Erratics

Distribution in Europe

Cabrera's vole *Microtus cabrerae* — Spain only

| | | | | | | | ● | | | |

Muskrat *Ondatra zibethicus* — northern central, central and eastern Europe

| | | | | | | | | ● | | ● |

Family Muridae

Striped field mouse *Apodemus agrarius* — northern Germany and southern Denmark eastwards to Russia

| ● | ● | ● | ● | ● | ● | ● | ● | ● | |

(fringes of woods — under Broadleaved/Mixed)

Harvest mouse *Micromys minutus* — whole continent except for north, Alps and most of Mediterranean region

| ● | ● | ● | ● | | | | ● | | |

Yellow-necked field mouse *Apodemus flavicollis* — central and eastern Europe north to Scandinavia and Finland, south to southern France and Greece, also southern Britain

| | | ● | ● | ● | ● | | | | |

Common field, Longtailed field or Wood mouse *Apodemus sylvaticus* — whole continent but north to southern Scandinavia

| ● | ● | | ● | ● | ● | | | | |

(fringes of woods — under Broadleaved/Mixed)

Broad-toothed field mouse or Rock mouse *Apodemus mystacinus* — Balkans only

| | | | ● | ● | | | | | |

Black or Ship rat *Rattus rattus* — localized

| | | ● | | | | | | | |

Brown or Common rat *Rattus norvegicus* — whole continent

| ● | ● | ● | ● | ● | | | | | |

House mouse *Mus musculus* — whole continent

| ● | ● | ● | ● | ● | | | | | |

Cairo spiny mouse *Acomys cahirinus* — Crete, Cyprus: introduced

| | | | | | | | | | ● |

Family Spalacidae

Lesser mole rat *Spalax leucodon* — southeastern Europe

| ● | ● | | | | | | | | |

Russian or Greater mole rat *Spalax microphthalmus* — southern Russia

| ● | ● | | | | | | | | |

		Pure steppes	Scrub, bush or wooded steppes	Human habitations	Broadleaved woodlands	Mixed woodlands	Coniferous forests	Mountains	Wetlands	Subarctic	Erratics
Distribution in Europe											
Family Zapodidae											
Northern birch mouse *Sicista betulina*	discontinuous and localized in northern, central and eastern Europe		●		●	●	●	●	●		
Southern birch mouse *Sicista subtilis*	southeastern Europe excluding Balkans		●		●	●	fringes only				
Family Hystricidae											
Crested porcupine *Hystrix cristata*	Italy, Sicily, parts of Yugoslavia: introduced			●							●
Family Myocastoridae											
Coypu or Nutria *Myocastor coypus*	western Europe: introduced								●		●
ORDER CARNIVORA											
Family Canidae											
Wolf *Canis lupus*	mainly in far north and in eastern Europe; elsewhere very localized				●	●	●	●		●	
Golden or Indian jackal *Canis aureus*	Balkans and Hungary only	●	●					●			
Arctic fox *Alopex lagopus*	far north									●	
Red fox *Vulpes vulpes*	whole continent		●		●	●	●				
Raccoon dog *Nyctereutes procyonoides*	Russia, northeastern Europe: introduced										●
Family Ursidae											
Brown bear *Ursus arctos*	in small numbers on mountain ranges throughout the continent						●	●			
Polar bear *Thalarctos maritimus*	coastal areas only									●	
Family Procyonidae											
Raccoon *Procyon lotor*	Germany and Russia only: introduced										●

	Pure steppes	Scrub, bush or wooded steppes	Human habitations	Broadleaved woodlands	Mixed woodlands	Coniferous forests	Mountains	Wetlands	Subarctic	Erratics

Distribution in Europe

Family Mustelidae

Species	Distribution in Europe	Pure steppes	Scrub, bush or wooded steppes	Human habitations	Broadleaved woodlands	Mixed woodlands	Coniferous forests	Mountains	Wetlands	Subarctic	Erratics
Badger *Meles meles*	whole of continent except Corsica, Sardinia and parts of Finland				●	●		●			
Stoat or Ermine *Mustela erminea*	absent only from Mediterranean Europe (including most of Iberia and Balkans)				●	●					
Weasel *Mustela nivalis*	whole continent except Ireland	●	●	●	●	●		●			
European mink *Mustela lutreola*	France and eastern Europe only (formerly more widespread)								●		
American mink *Mustela vison*	Russia, Finland, Scandinavia, Germany, Britain introduced								●		●
European polecat *Putorius putorius*	whole continent except most of Scandinavia and Finland, most of British Isles, Balkans and Mediterranean islands		●		●	●					
Marbled polecat *Vormela peregusna*	almost entirely confined to Rumania and Bulgaria	●			●	●					
Common otter *Lutra lutra*	whole continent except Corsica and Sardinia								●		
Pine marten *Martes martes*	most of Europe except Britain (only small populations in Wales and Scotland), the Low Countries, most of Iberia and Balkans and Corsica				●	●	●				
Beech or Stone marten *Martes foina*	whole of continent except Scandinavia to northern Russia, British Isles, Corsica, Sardinia, Sicily	●	●		● (fringes of woods)	●	●	●			
Sable *Martes zibellina*	extreme north of Scandinavia to northern Russia only					●	●				

	Pure steppes	Scrub, bush or wooded steppes	Human habitations	Broadleaved woodlands	Mixed woodlands	Coniferous forests	Mountains	Wetlands	Subarctic	Erratics
Glutton or Wolverine *Gulo gulo* — extreme north (including much of Scandinavia) only					●	●	●	●		
Family Viverridae										
Egyptian mongoose or Ichneumon *Herpestes ichneumon* — southern Iberia only: introduced							●			●
European, Feline or Small-spotted genet *Genetta genetta* — Iberia, central and southern France only: introduced					●	●				●
Family Felidae										
European wild cat *Felis silvestris* — discontinuous distribution, mainly in central and southern Europe and Scottish highlands	●				●	●				
Lynx or Northern lynx *Lynx lynx* — discontinuous distribution in northern and eastern Europe					●	●	●			
Pardel or Spanish lynx *Lynx pardina* — Iberia, Carpathians, Balkans						●	●			
ORDER ARTIODACTYLA										
Family Suidae										
Wild boar *Sus scrofa* — whole continent except British Isles and the north generally; not in Sicily					●	●				
Family Cervidae										
Chinese water deer *Hydropotes inermis* — England and France only: introduced										●
Chinese or Reeve's muntjac *Muntiacus reevesi* — England and France only: introduced										●
Fallow deer *Dama dama* — whole continent but localized (distribution affected by extermination and re-introduction)				●	●	●				
Red deer *Cervus elaphus* — widespread over whole continent but in places localized; absent Ireland, Corsica, Sardinia, Sicily				●	●	●				

Distribution in Europe

	Distribution in Europe	Pure steppes	Scrub, bush or wooded steppes	Human habitations	Broadleaved woodlands	Mixed woodlands	Coniferous forests	Mountains	Wetlands	Subarctic	Erratics
Sika deer *Cervus nippon*	Britain, France, Denmark, Germany: introduced				●	●	●				●
Roe deer *Capreolus capreolus*	whole continent except extreme north, Ireland and Mediterranean islands		●		●	●	●				
Elk *Alces alces*	Scandinavia, Finland, northern Russia, but extending range southwards and westwards				●	●			● summer		
White-tailed or Virginian deer *Odocoileus virginianus*	feral in southwest Finland only										●
Reindeer *Rangifer tarandus*	northern Scandinavia, Finland, northern Russia: introduced Scotland									●	
Family Bovidae											
European bison or Wisent *Bison bonasus*	Poland only					●					
Mouflon *Ovis musimon*	Corsica and Sardinia only; elsewhere introduced							●			
Ibex or Wild goat *Capra hircus*	southern Europe only							●			
Chamois *Rupicapra rupicapra*	southern and central Europe							●			
Musk-ox *Ovibos moschatus*	introduced (Norway)									●	●
Saiga *Saiga tatarica*	southern Russia	●	●								●

ORDER PINNIPEDIA

	Arctic	Temperate	Mediterranean	Cosmopolitan
Family Phocidae				
Common or Harbor seal *Phoca vitulina*		●		
Harp seal *Pagophilus groenlandicus*	●			
Bearded seal *Erignathus barbatus*	●			
Ringed seal *Pusa hispida*	●			
Grey or Atlantic seal *Halichoerus grypus*		●		
Hooded seal *Cystophora cristata*	●			
Monk seal *Monachus monachus*			●	
Family Odobenidae				
Walrus *Odobenus rosmarus*	●			

ORDER CETACEA

	Arctic	Temperate	Mediterranean	Cosmopolitan
Family Balaenopteridae				
Blue Whale *Balaenoptera musculus*		●		
Fin whale or Common rorqual *Balaenoptera physalus*		●		
Sei whale *Balaenoptera borealis*		●		
Minke whale or Lesser rorqual *Balaenoptera acutorostrata*		●		
Humpback whale *Megaptera novaeangliae*		●		
Family Balaenidae				
Greenland right whale or Bonehead *Balaena mysticetus*	●			
Biscayan or North Atlantic right whale *Eubalaena glacialis*	●			
Family Physeteridae				
Sperm whale *Physeter catodon*				●
Pygmy sperm whale *Kogia breviceps*				●
Family Ziphiidae				
Bottlenosed whale *Hyperoodon rostratus*		●		
Beaked or True's whale *Mesoplodon mirus*		●		
Sowerby's whale *Mesoplodon bidens*		●		
Cuvier's beaked or Goose-beaked whale *Ziphius cavirostris*				●
Family Monodontidae				
Narwhal *Monodon monoceros*	●			
Beluga or White whale *Delphinapterus leucas*	●			
Family Delphinidae				
Killer whale *Orcinus orca*				●
False killer *Pseudorca crassidens*				●
Risso's dolphin *Grampus griseus*				●
Pilot or Caa'ling whale *Globicephala melaena*				●
Common dolphin *Delphinus delphis*				●
Bottlenosed dolphin *Tursiops truncatus*				●
White-sided dolphin *Lagenorhynchus acutus*		●		
White-beaked dolphin *Lagenorhynchus albirostris*		●		
Rough-toothed dolphin *Steno bredanensis*				●
Striped dolphin *Stenella coeruleoalba*				●
Family Phocaenidae				
Common porpoise *Phocoena phocoena*				●

PURE STEPPES

The word steppe is derived from the Russian *stepi* and, in its strictest sense, describes the open, grassy plains of the temperate zone of Eurasia between the latitudes 40°N and 50°N, from the Danube Basin in the west, eastwards to the valley of the River Yenisei in central Siberia and the continental highlands of Mongolia and China. The climate is typically continental with winter temperatures remaining well below freezing point for at least four months when permanent snow cover exceeds 100mm (4in), and high summer temperatures which, together with an absence of summer rainfall, often cause late summer drought. As a result of these extremes, steppe is essentially treeless.

The steppe soils are all varieties of types called chernozem or chestnut. They are derived from loess, particles deposited on the ground surface by the wind during dry spells. Chernozem soils have a black surface layer of humus often up to 150cm (60in) in depth, are generally poor in carbonates and lack clay. Chestnut soils have a low humus content and are consequently brown in colour with a paler, alkaline horizon of salt accumulation formed by the wash-

ing down of salt particles, deposited on the soil surface by summer winds from the deserts to the south, by spring snow-melt water. These soils are ideally suited to the feather-grasses that dominate the vegetation of pure steppe: members of the genus *Stipa*. These grasses grow and develop as the snow cover melts in mid-April. In the meadow-steppe, a variety of colourful spring herbs flower until mid-May as the temperature rises and while the soil is still damp. Towards the end of May, the long awns of the feather-grasses appear, and the swaying of the plumes against a profusion of colour is a typical sight until July when rainfall ceases and the vegetation starts to wither. By the drought period of August, the steppes have assumed a dry and barren appearance in which form they stay until the snow cover returns in November.

In the Volga basin, a variety of steppe occurs called dry steppe. This region is dominated by low growing feather-grasses and sheep's fescue. These plants survive where the climate is dry and evaporation exceeds rainfall by 300–500mm (12–20in). In some places vegetation is ex-

tremely sparse and huge areas of bare soil occur in which there is little protection from the summer heat.

The effects of man's activities in steppe regions have been considerable, at least in some areas. The most ancient and perhaps the most important influence on vegetation has been through the use of fire and, though fires are occasionally started by natural agents, it seems that many grasslands owe their origin and existence to deliberate firing. Evidence from pollen analysis of peat deposits in northwestern Europe indicates that forest destruction and grassland establishment were well advanced by 2500 BC. Burning kills off old growth and rapidly releases nutrients back to the soil. The grasses found in steppe regions are well adapted to burning;

43

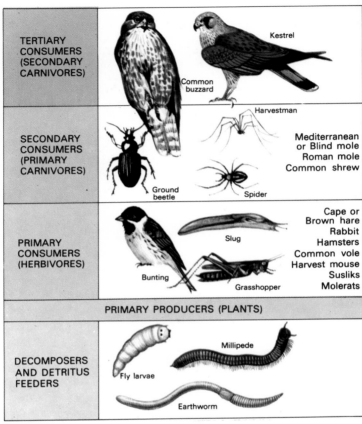

TERTIARY CONSUMERS (SECONDARY CARNIVORES)	Kestrel, Common buzzard
SECONDARY CONSUMERS (PRIMARY CARNIVORES)	Harvestman, Ground beetle, Spider, Mediterranean or Blind mole, Roman mole, Common shrew
PRIMARY CONSUMERS (HERBIVORES)	Bunting, Slug, Grasshopper, Cape or Brown hare, Rabbit, Hamsters, Common vole, Harvest mouse, Susliks, Molerats
PRIMARY PRODUCERS (PLANTS)	
DECOMPOSERS AND DETRITUS FEEDERS	Fly larvae, Millipede, Earthworm

the buds for next season's growth are normally close to the ground and protected by a dense mass of dead leaves.

Feeding relationships. Because pure steppe is predominantly grassland, the invertebrate fauna is dominated by earthworms, particularly species of the genus *Allolobophora*. Living in the upper surface of the soil, they are primarily decomposers, feeding on dead plant material. In this they are assisted by populations of millipedes and some dipteran fly larvae. Larger units of dead organic matter such as occasional woody material and animal detritus are degraded by woodlice, lice and nematodes (roundworms).

The predatory mammal populations are purely primary carnivores surviving to a great extent on the dense earthworm and herbivorous insect communities. Lack of diversity in the insect community, which is composed mainly of grasshoppers and wideranging carabid beetles, has led to the establishment of a single insectivorous mammal, the Common shrew. This species competes, however, with the Blind and Roman moles where their ranges overlap.

Low vegetation cover and lack of nesting sites has prohibited the spread of secondary carnivorous mammals such as the mustelids (Weasels and polecats) and jackals found in scrub and bush steppe. Predation is merely by long-range accipiters, for example Common buzzards, which fly out effortlessly from wooded vantage points to feeding areas using air currents to glide long distances.

The bulk of the mammal population is made up of herbivores which avoid direct competition with each other by feeding on different foodstuffs. Hares, Rabbits and susliks feed mainly on leaf blades, voles on stem bases and Mole rats, hamsters and Harvest mice on seeds, though Hamsters occasionally take small birds. The Mole rats show strong parallel evolution of behaviour with the moles, using their incisor teeth to dig in the same way as mole forelimbs.

Common shrews fighting.

COMMON SHREW

ORDER	Insectivora
FAMILY	Soricidae
GENUS	Sorex
SPECIES	S. araneus

Description: small, mouse-like, with coat of close, silky fur, dark brown to almost black on upperparts, paling to dirty yellowish-grey below. Thin, tapering bilobed snout and long whiskers, extending far beyond mouth. Teeth red-tipped. Hairy feet flesh-coloured. Hindfoot just over 15mm ($\frac{1}{2}$in). Tail dark above, light below, covered with short, stiff, spine-like hairs. Sometimes tail white-tipped and white ear-tufts not uncommon. Lateral glands midway between elbow and thigh give out musky odour. Two moults: one in autumn leaving a long coat, second in spring leaving short coat. Moult starts on hindquarters and moves forward to head. Records of albinos, melanics and sandy-coloured individuals and also normal coats with white spots and patches. Head and body length 70–85mm (3–3$\frac{1}{2}$in). Tail length varies considerably but usually about half head and body length. Weight averages 8–12g ($\frac{1}{3}$oz). Increase of growth at sexual maturity.

46

Range: throughout Europe except for most of Iberian Peninsula and Mediterranean islands. Extends eastwards through Asia to Pacific, northwards to tundra, often to Arctic Ocean. Sea level to 450m (1500ft).

Habitat: wherever there is ground cover, especially in long grass; also hedgerows, ditch-sides, woodlands, heather moors, mountain scree.

Life history: breeding season May to September in north and to October in south. Gestation probably 13–21 days. Occasional resorption of embryos. 3 or more litters a year of 4–10 young (average 6). Newly-born weigh 0·5g ($\frac{1}{100}$oz). Eyes open 18–21 days, weaned two days later. Small percentage of females in first litters may become sexually mature in year of birth if food abundant but usually young mature during the year after birth. Longevity 15 months.

Feeding: feeds mainly below surface or in leaf litter. Consumes $\frac{3}{4}$ of own weight of food in a day, nursing female $1\frac{1}{2}$ times. Snout used for turning over dead leaves and loose surface soil for food. Surplus food stored. Food: soil insects, worms, snails, spiders, woodlice, Carrion taken, if fresh, including other shrews.

Habits: solitary except in breeding season. Each 24 hours divided into 10 periods of activity, alternating with slightly shorter periods of rest. Peaks of activity mid-morning and late evening; drop in activity mid-afternoon. Activity more intense during night. Winter spent among leaf litter but no hibernation. In summer runways made through grass; tunnels of mice or moles sometimes used. Will climb stout grass stems after insects, and may climb to 2·4m (8ft) up trees. Will burrow quickly into light or loosened soil, using forefeet. Pebbles removed with mouth. Swims readily. Aggressive, fighting among selves when numbers high, but usually only posturing and screaming to drive away intruder. Nests woven of grasses into cup-shape, below ground, in banks of ditches or on surface under cover. Sleeping nest less substantial.

Voice a soft twittering when exploring. Shrill screaming in aggression.

Many predators refuse to eat

Common shrew *Sorex araneus*.

shrew because of musky odour and unpalatable flesh. Cats kill but do not eat them. Owls main predators, also other birds of prey (eg Kestrel), magpies, jackdaws, Stoats, vipers and smooth snakes will take them.

Populations: peak numbers usually June to August, lowest numbers towards end of winter. Heavy mor-tality (25 %) of young in first four months.

Special features: movements rapid and bustling exploring busily with snout and whiskers, now and again rearing up to sniff air. Touch, hearing and probably kinaesthetic sense more important than sight and hearing.

COMMON MOLE

ORDER	Insectivora
FAMILY	Talpidae
GENUS	*Talpa*
SPECIES	*T. europaea*

Description: dark grey fur cover-ing body appears black, is without set. Body cylindrical, no perceptible neck. Forelimbs set well forward, hands with five digits, large and broad, wide open, palms always face outwards. Strong claws on fore-limbs. Hindlimbs weaker. Muzzle pointed; eyes tiny, usually hidden by erect hair; ear without external pinna. Tail stumpy, narrow at base, carried vertically. Scattered bristle-like hairs over snout and head, richly supplied with nerves and blood vessels at roots. Three moults, spring, July to September, early Oc-tober to December. Occasional vari-ations in colour, cream, orange-pink, whitish-black, sometimes orange or yellowish markings on normal skins, other skins wholly grey, fawn or ash-coloured. Albinos occasionally. Size varies from one locality to another and from year to year. Average male: head and body length 140mm (5½in). Females slightly smaller. In both tail about 32mm (1¼in). Weight at maximum from February to April. Average for male nearly 110g (4oz), for female nearly 85g (3oz).

Range: across Europe (except parts of south and north) and Asia (south to Himalayas, north to Altai Moun-tains but not Japan).

Habitat: spends almost entire life in tunnels from few inches to a few feet below ground. Almost every habitat except barren mountains, sand and conifer forests. Usually in open ground, in permanent pasture, arable land, gardens and parks.

Life history: boar and sow appear to associate only temporarily. Female polyandrous. Mating season end of March and beginning of April. Gestation probably about 4 weeks (possibly 5–6 weeks). Litter 2–7, usually 3–4 (higher numbers in Russia). One litter a year, second litter rare. Reproduction controlled by resorption of foetuses. Young born blind, naked and pink. Weight at birth 3·5g (⅛oz). At 2 weeks skin darkens to a bluish-slate, then fur begins to grow. Eyes open 22nd day when weight over 60g (2oz). Young, which already appear like adults, leave nest at about 5 weeks,

Common mole *Talpa europaea.*

then travel considerable distances overland, probably forced onto surface by adults. Sexually mature in February of following year. Longevity 3 years.

Feeding: diet almost confined to soil fauna. No need to drink when feeding on earthworms. Single mole eats 18–36kg (40–80lb) in a year. Will die of starvation if without food for few hours, so earthworms stored when abundant. Head bitten off, rest stored. If not needed for food, worm grows another head and burrows away. Much of food taken when prey burrows through walls of tunnels, so reduces need for mole to dig for food, occasionally prey taken above ground. When eating earthworm mole holds it in forepaws and pulls with jaws, with hind-feet set wide and bracing body. Food includes earthworms, beetle and fly larvae, predominantly. Myriapods and molluscs (mainly slugs) constant but not so commonly. Occasionally vegetable matter. Said to break open and eat eggs, even of domestic fowl.

Habits: nests for resting made from any dry material (eg dead leaves and grass) built in runway system. Alternation of $4\frac{1}{2}$ hours activity with $3\frac{1}{2}$ hours rest throughout 24 hours. Periods in nest involve deep sleep on all fours, head tucked between forelimbs. Breeding nest about 300mm (1ft) in diameter made of grass, leaves or twigs sometimes under earth mound sheltered by bush or tree.

Voice a twittering sound, fast snuffling action, when excited. Also high-pitched squeal, possibly lower range of ultrasonics. Sounds made when chewing and sound of breathing resembling rapid sniffing when exploring habitat may aid in general echo-location.

Predators: Tawny and Barn owls, rats, Stoats, Weasels, Foxes, Badgers, cats and herons. In eastern Europe moles form considerable proportion of food of Pine martens. May form nearly 50% of Tawny owl's food in summer when young come above ground.

Question whether moles valuable or detrimental to agriculture. They aerate and drain soil with burrows but stones on molehills blunt blades of farm machines.

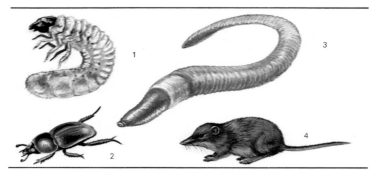

Food of the Common mole: (1) larvae and (2) adult beetles. (3) earthworms and (4) occasional small mammals.

Special features: each burrow system belongs to a single individual. Both sexes have branching systems but males have long straight runs especially in spring, although both sexes appear to use same main tunnels. Home range in pasture

Burrowing activity of moles results in the formation of mole-hills on the surface.

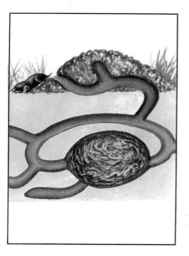

27–36m (30–40yd) for females; males 45m (50yd) in winter, 138m (153yd) in spring. Burrows mainly same diameter as mole, which squeezes fur clean as it travels along. Deeper burrows 305–610mm (1–2ft) down indicated by molehills; shallow burrows visible as ridges on surface. Simple open furrows sometimes found.

Forelimbs used for excavating, hands used alternately and also used to push earth onto surface. Locomotion by sideways thrusts of forelimbs; said to travel backwards using hind-limbs only. Speed of travel above ground and below between 4 and 5 kph (2½–3 mph). Swims well at about same speed.

Senses: mole's eye, although tiny, perfectly constructed. Probably can see stationary objects but is slow to see. Sight not very important. Reacts to wide range of sounds. Probable ability to appreciate vibrations through ground. Sense of smell not so acute as once thought. Touch most important sense. Tactile hairs on chin and muzzle; top of muzzle hairs highly sensitive receptors. Sensitive hairs on tip of tail. Numerous small special organs of touch in skin.

MEDITERRANEAN OR BLIND MOLE

ORDER	Insectivora
FAMILY	Talpidae
GENUS	*Talpa*
SPECIES	*T. caeca*

Description: similar in habits, habitat and appearance to common

Blind mole *Talpa caeca*.

mole, slightly smaller, head and body 95—140mm (4—4¾in), with light, nearly white, hairs on snout-tip and front legs, bare area of snout longer and narrower. Eyes often hidden under skin. Fewer mole-hills thrown up on surface because tunnels not so deep. Ranges Iberian Peninsula, southern half of France, northern half of Italy, through Dalmatia to most of Greece.

ROMAN MOLE

ORDER	Insectivora
FAMILY	Talpidae
GENUS	*Talpa*
SPECIES	*T. romana*

Description: similar in appearance to Blind mole but slightly larger (head and body 126—165mm (5—5½in)). Range includes southern Italy, Sicily, Corfu and Greece. (The Roman mole is sometimes considered to be a subspecies of the Mole *T. europaea*).

RABBIT

ORDER	Lagomorpha
FAMILY	Oryctolagidae
GENUS	*Oryctolagus*
SPECIES	*O. cuniculus*

Description: sexes similar but doe smaller and has longer, more delicately moulded head than buck. Coat made up of three kinds of hairs: dense, soft woolly underfur through which project longer and stronger hairs giving coat its colour, and longer but more sparse hairs scattered among these; becomes thicker in winter. Mainly buff sprinkled with black, nape blackish, underparts whitish; tail black above, white below. Much colour variation from light sandy to black. Black rabbits and, more rarely, other colour mutants turn up occasionally in wild. On islands and other closed communities, genes for colour variation, swamped in open communities, have more chance to emerge. Ears long, eyes large and prominent, placed well to sides of head. Hind

Rabbit *Oryctolagus cuniculus.*

legs longer than front legs and strongly developed for bounding run. Soles covered with thick coating of hair giving firm grip on hard rock or slippery snow. Tail very short and turned up. Glands under chin with secretion for marking territory. Adult head and body length up to 400mm (16in). Weight up to 2kg (4½lb).

Range: Europe, north to southern Sweden, east to Poland and Crete, south and west to North Africa and Atlantic Islands. 6 subspecies. Introduced Australia, New Zealand, United States, Chile etc.

Habitat: abundant in grassland, woodlands, cultivated fields. Also sand-dune, salt marsh, mountains, moorlands or cliffs.

Life history: polygamous, one buck mating with several does, each doe keeping to own territory in warren. Mating preceded by complicated courtship, in which buck chases doe. Sometimes two bucks fight (formalized). Litters of 2–8, higher numbers in warmer months, at intervals of a month from January to June, some sporadic breeding in other months. Gestation 28 days. Percentage of embryos resorbed. Young born blind, deaf (ears closed) and almost naked. Ears open 10th day, eyes 11th day. Few days later can run and come out of nest. Take solid food 16 days, weaned 30 days. Meanwhile mother defends them using powerful hindfeet against adversary. Sexually mature at 3 to 4 months; growth continues to 9 months.

Feeding: almost exclusively vegetarian. Chief food grass and tender shoots of furze. Agricultural crops devastated, cereals, roots, pastures, garden crops and young trees. Can eat 0·45kg (1lb) or more of fresh green food daily. Can convert ling heath to grassland and downland to scrub. Occasionally eats snails and earthworms. Special latrines used. Voids two types of droppings, one kind eaten again (refection), the other discarded at latrine.

Habits: usually live in warrens (strictly should be called buries), consisting of short tunnels or complicated burrow systems, some going down as much as 2·7m (9ft). Residential quarters are always blind chambers leading from main passages. Young usually born in 'stab' or 'stop', a short burrow about 61cm (2ft) long, just under surface, well away from main burrow, nest being in blind end. Some young born in nests on surface. Adult Rabbits use no nesting materials, rest on bare soil, but pregnant doe makes bed for young of hay or straw lined with fur stripped from underparts. Mainly crepuscular and nocturnal but if undisturbed, also diurnal.

Normally silent except for occasional low growls and grunts when alarmed or content. Low notes from doe when nursing young. Loud scream when attack by Stoat imminent. Thump on ground with both hind feet together used as alarm signal to colony, usually given by an old buck.

Apart from man, predators include members of weasel family, owls, buzzards, ravens, crows, Black-

Rabbits are born blind and naked (1) and can see only after 11 days (2).

backed gulls, variety of hawks, also fox, Wild and feral cats and feral dogs. Badgers dig out young.

Populations: before 1954 Rabbit

Rabbits feeding.

53

a pest in Europe (60–100 million in Great Britain alone) and wherever introduced. Populations greatly reduced by myxomatosis in 1954/5. Show signs of recovery now. Numbers at maximum May to June. Even where no predation numbers fall to normal by following spring (due to disease, accident, neglect etc).

Special features: can swim but climbs indifferently. Sprints and dodges rapidly. Digs well in light soil, but sometimes in firm loam or clay and even into surface of coal. Instinct to dig present from an early age, and survives domestication. Travels up to 1·5km (1 mile) for food but no evidence of migration.

CAPE OR BROWN HARE

ORDER	Lagomorpha
FAMILY	Leporidae
GENUS	*Lepus*
SPECIES	*L. capensis*

Description: similar in form and structure to closely related Rabbit, differs in having longer body, longer hindlimbs, longer ears with black tips and tawny fur on upperparts. Shoulders, neck and flanks of ruddier hue than back. Back a mixture of grey and brown. Underside white. Breast, loins ruddy. Profusion of black and white whiskers, white being longer. Tail carried curved over back or straight behind, black above and white on sides and below. Large prominent eyes on sides of head with horizontal pupil. Male or Jack has smaller body, shorter head and

Brown hare *Lepus capensis*.

redder shoulders than doe. Moult twice a year. Spring moult, protracted and more gradual, February to June or July. Autumn moult starts soon after spring moult has ended. No great difference between winter and summer coats although former may be more grey; latter reddish with grey patches, especially on hindquarters. Both moults start along back, go down flanks and limbs and finish at head and tail. Total length 610mm (24in), weight (average) 3·6kg (8lb).

Brown hare in its form.

Range: Europe from southern Finland and Sweden to Mediterranean, then eastwards into western Asia and Asia Minor and Persia. Also throughout Africa. Introduced Australia, New Zealand etc.

Habitat: open ground, moorland, arable farmland, rough pasture especially downland, marshes, woodlands, aerodromes. Up to 600m (2000ft) or more.

Life history: courtship includes aggressive behaviour of males (boxing, chasing, leaping etc) in groups, reaching peak in early spring (Mad March Hares). Breeding season variable in different parts of range, but everywhere capable of breeding all year round. Gestation 42—44 days. Superfoetation known. 3—4 litters a year, each of 2—4, occasionally more. Heavy mortality among embryos, which are resorbed, especially in autumn. Form made in rank grass in open field. Young born with eyes open and a short, furry coat, lacking ruddiness of adult. Capable of using limbs soon after birth. Able to occupy own 'form' in vicinity of that of mother. Doe visits each leveret in turn to suckle it. Uses bounding tactics in doing so, leaving no telltale scent-trail. Leverets fully independent at month old, reach sexual maturity at eight months, do not breed in first year.

Feeding: from early evening to early morning in open country. Destructive to young trees in plantations. May be pest on farms and market gardens. Home range 1·5 to 3km (1 to 2 miles). May travel many miles in night to feed (one tracked 30 miles). Food: bark, grain, roots, herbaceous vegetation, carrots, lettuce, turnips and other vegetables, grasses, clover, sowthistle and chicory, flowers in private gardens, fungi, voles. Refection as in Rabbits.

Habits: normally solitary, resting place during day a slight depression in long grass known as a 'form'. Same form may be used over a period. Doe makes no special nursery but uses same or similar resting form. Relies for security on speed, or on crouching in low vegetation. On leaving form makes prodigious leap, 4·5m (15ft) or more. When hotly pursued jinks and doubles on tracks to confuse enemy. Good swimmer, will cross river 183m (200yd) wide to reach feeding ground.

Voice shrill. If wounded or badly scared screams like child in pain. Warning sound made by grinding teeth, passed from hare to hare, serves same purpose probably as stamping of hindfeet by rabbit. Courtship notes of buck and doe different and their imitation by poachers and gamekeepers is known as sucking.

Adults may be taken by foxes, Wild cats and eagles, Stoats and medium-sized birds of prey but these usually prey mainly on leverets. Possibility that Rabbits attack hares. Doe will fight if leverets disturbed or attacked. Hunted by man.

Populations: alternating periods of abundance and scarcity (latter often accompanied by disease coccidiosis). In Finland large numbers die in winters with deep snow. Great Britain density 1 per 4 hectares (10ac) (1956). France density 1 per 1 hectare (2·5ac) (1958).

Senses: wide field of vision — eyes on sides of head.

EUROPEAN SUSLIK

ORDER	Rodentia
FAMILY	Sciuridae
GENUS	*Citellus*
SPECIES	*C. citellus*

Description: ground squirrel with relatively short legs and tail and small rounded ears. Fur slightly coarse, greyish-brown, usually without spots or only indistinctly spotted, white or yellowish under-parts. Head and body length 192 to 220mm (8—9in), tail 55—75mm (2—3in), weight 240 to 340g ($8\frac{1}{2}$—12oz).

Range: eastern central Europe, south-eastwards to shores of Aegean Sea.

Food of the European suslik: (1) seeds, (2) eggs, (3) grass, (4) fruit, (5) insects and (6) young birds.

Habitat: typically dry steppes but also meadows and fields, usually in

European suslik *Citellus citellus*.

plains but also goes high up in mountains.

Life history: gestation 23–28 days. One litter a year of 2–13 young born naked, blind and toothless. These leave the nest at the age of one month.

Feeding: active by day searching for seeds, nuts, roots, bulbs, green stems and leaves. Also eats insects, small birds and eggs and mice. Quantities of seeds and nuts carried in internal cheek pouches for storing underground.

Habits: very like those of better known Prairie dogs of North America. Diurnal but especially active at dawn and in evening. Live in loose communities, in burrows they dig themselves. Burrows sometimes complicated systems of tunnels, deep in ground, often with several entrances including one leading vertically downwards. Habit of sitting erect on haunches to keep watch, or well up on hind legs to peer over a rock. Hibernates in northern parts of range. Voice soft giving plaintive singing sounds turning to abrupt whistle when alarmed or excited. Also growling followed by a sigh accompanied by head-nodding.

SPOTTED SUSLIK

ORDER	Rodentia
FAMILY	Sciuridae
GENUS	*Citellus*
SPECIES	*C. suslicus*

Description: similar to European suslik in habitat, habits and appearance except that coat is distinctly spotted with white and tail markedly shorter.

Range: steppes of southern Russia.

Special features: around two hundred holes in ground, dug by Spotted susliks, have been counted in a single acre (400sq m) of land. Preyed upon by Black kite. Mates soon after waking from hibernation.

COMMON HAMSTER

ORDER	Rodentia
FAMILY	Cricetidae
GENUS	*Cricetus*
SPECIES	*C. cricetus*

Description: largest species of hamster, size of Guinea pig. Thick fur, light brown above, black below, with white patches on sides. Short but conspicuous tail. Feet broad, usually with well-developed claws. Large cheek pouches. Lateral glands with secretions for marking territory. Almost black mutant occurs. Head and body length 215–320mm (8½–12in), tail 28–60mm (1–2¼in), weight 150–385g (5⅓–13½oz).

Range: Central and eastern Europe (Belgium to Caucasus).

Habitat: ploughed fields, cultivated land, grassland, along river banks.

Life history: breeding season April to August. Gestation 19–20 days. Usually 2 litters a year with 6–12 young born naked and blind. Weaned three weeks, immediately leaving mother. Breed in following spring.

Common hamster showing cheek pouches.

58

Feeding: mainly vegetarian. Seeds, including cereal grain, main food. Also roots, potatoes, insects, frogs. Has become agricultural pest. Food collected in cheek pouches and carried back to nest. Large winter food stores in burrows.

Habits: nocturnal but occasionally comes out by day. Sleeps and stores food in burrows. Short, shallow burrows in summer, extensive with several entrances and compartments

Common hamster *Cricetus cricetus*.

for nesting, storing food and latrines. Hibernates during winter in deeper burrows but wakes at intervals to feed from large food stores: 45kg (100lb) of seeds and potatoes recorded. Does not build up layer of body fat before hibernation but stimulated to store food by cold weather. Solitary except in breeding season. Swims often, inflating cheek pouches to give extra buoyancy.

GOLDEN HAMSTER

ORDER	Rodentia
FAMILY	Cricetidae
GENUS	*Mesocricetus*
SPECIES	*M. auratus*

Description: stocky, short-legged, with blunt snout, moderately large ears and eyes, light-reddish brown above, white or cream underparts. Females slightly larger than males. Skin of body loose especially over

cheek pouches, which open inside mouth and extend backwards under skin over shoulders. When pouches filled they more than double width of head. There are 14–16 mammae and this, as well as smaller body size dis-

Golden hamster *Mesocricetus auratus* (1) and Grey or Migratory hamster *Cricetulus migratorius* (2).

tinguishes this species from Common hamster. Head and body length 170–180mm (6½in), tail 12mm (½in) long, weight up to 130g (4½oz).

Range: Rumania, Bulgaria, Israel and northwest Iran.

Habitat: sandy steppes and brush-covered slopes.

Life history: gestation 15–19 days, several litters a year of 4–15

(6–7 usually) young born helpless, naked, blind. Weaned at three weeks. Capable of breeding at 8–10 weeks. Longevity 2–3 years.

Habits: mainly nocturnal, usually solitary, defend themselves when alarmed but readily tamed and docile. Burrowing, stores food in burrow transported there in capacious cheek pouches.

Special features: all pet hamsters descended from mother and 12 offspring which were dug out of the Syrian desert in 1930 and taken to Israel.

COMMON VOLE

ORDER	Rodentia
FAMILY	Muridae
GENUS	*Microtus*
SPECIES	*M. arvalis*

Description: short-haired smooth coat, sandy-brown above, lighter below. Subspecies on Orkney and Guernsey larger and darker. Almost unicoloured tail. Small, nearly naked ears. Head and body length 83–120mm (3¼–4¾in), tail 30–45mm (1¼–1¾in), weight 14–46g (½–1½oz).

Range: most of Europe, but absent

from Scandinavia, Finland, most of lowland Iberia, Italy and Balkans. Absent from British Isles except Orkney and Guernsey.

Habitat: cultivated land; grazed pastures, meadows, orchards.

Life history: breeds March to October. Gestation 21 days. Several

Common vole *Microtus arvalis*.

Bark of an apple tree gnawed away by Common vole.

litters a year of 3–6 young. Weaned and independent at 14–18 days, sexually mature at 3 weeks, mate at 6 weeks.

Feeding: grass, roots, cultivated crops. Can do considerable economic damage.

Habits: probably active day and night but especially at dusk. Runs fast, swims well. Makes short shallow tunnels underground with nesting chambers and storerooms. Nests in tunnel or sometimes above ground. Voice a high chirping squeak, not often heard. Preyed upon especially by birds of prey such as Hen harrier, owls and also by any mammal or bird large enough to take it.

Populations: numbers may reach plague proportions in some years.

HARVEST MOUSE

ORDER	Rodentia
FAMILY	Muridae
GENUS	*Micromys*
SPECIES	*M. minutus*

Description: smallest European rodent. Thick soft fur of upper parts yellowish-red, underparts white, colours fairly sharply separated.

61

Hairless scaly tail, pliant with outer end prehensile. Short blunt snout, short rounded ears $\frac{1}{3}$ length of body. Outer of 5 toes of each hindfoot large and opposable to rest. Hindfeet and tail used for climbing grass and corn stems leaving front paws free for holding food. Head and body length 50–69mm (2–3in), tail 46–66mm (1·8–2·5in), weight 4–10g ($\frac{1}{8}$–$\frac{1}{4}$oz).

Range: western Europe to China but absent from most of Mediterranean and Scandinavia. Island populations in British Isles and Japan.

Habitat: pastures, cornfields, hedgerows, open fields, salt marshes, reed beds, dykes.

Life history: breeds April to September. Gestation 21 days. Several

Harvest mice *Micromys minutus*.

litters a year of 5 to 9 young. Eyes open 8 days. Excursions from nest at 11–12 days. Independent at 15 days at weight 5·5g. Reach adult weight in 24 days. Until December fur of young grey then from hindquarters forward assumes reddish tint. Longevity 18 months in wild (4 years recorded in captivity).

Feeding: seeds, fruits, buds, insects (in summer). Stores food in burrows for winter use.

Habits: active throughout day and night with three-hourly rhythm. Shelters during non-active periods in burrows in earth, or in hayricks. Breeding nest about 76mm (3in) in diameter, of woven blades of grass. Only female and young occupy nursery nest (male not allowed to enter), slung from several stout stems 60–300mm (2–12in) above ground, occasionally in branches of blackthorn bush or broom. Bed, made of leaves of corn or grass shredded longitudinally, in nest at ground level. Generally inoffensive and gentle, but said at times to become savage and cannibalistic. Lacks offensive odour.

Voice a low chirp, faint squeaks, bird-like chirruping during courtship.

Habitat affords good protection from avian predators but Tawny owl takes some. Smaller mustelids prey on them and perhaps also snakes.

Populations: variable in numbers even in neighbouring localities and from year to year. Numbers have decreased during last 100 years, in British Isles at least, possibly because of use of reaping machines. Revival in 1955. Probably was tolerably rare in Europe even before 18th century.

Vegetation shredded prior to weaving into the nest by Harvest mouse.

Nests of the Harvest mouse.

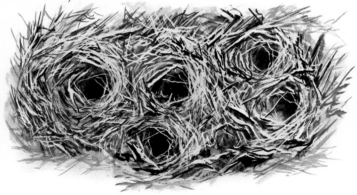

LESSER MOLE RAT

ORDER	Rodentia
FAMILY	Spalacidae
GENUS	*Spalax*
SPECIES	*S. leucodon*

Description: cylindrical mole-like body covered with soft velvety fur, sandy coloured, tinged with black on face and underparts. Legs very short, feet pink, with relatively small claws. Row of tactile bristles either side of head, which is marked by a white oblique line. Eyes vestigial, hidden under skin, external ears lacking. Tail vestigial. Head and body length 185—270mm (7½—10½in), weight 140—220g (5—7¾oz).

Range: Balkans, north to plains of Hungary.

Habitat: steppes and valleys, especially where soil cultivated.

Life history: mating November to January, gestation about a month, with one litter a year of 2—4 naked, pink young, each 50mm (2in) long, 5g (⅙oz) weight, born in underground nest of dried grass. Covered with long grey fur in two weeks. Leave nest at 4—6 weeks and then seen wandering over surface of ground in search of a territory.

Feeding: roots, bulbs, tubers and other underground parts of plants; grass, seeds and a few insects taken on rare emergence above ground.

Habits: solitary except in breeding season. Active mainly at night. Makes a tunnel system marked at intervals by small mounds of earth on surface, with 15—20 larger mounds near centre beneath each of which is a nursery nest or slightly smaller (250—350mm (10—14in) diameter) resting nests. Tunnel system includes special storage chambers

Lesser mole rat *Spalax leucodon*.

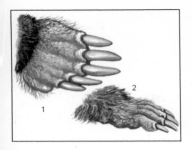

Foot of Common mole (1) compared with that of Lesser mole rat (2)

for food as well as latrine chambers. Digs with very large incisors assisted by special jaw structure, permitting greater backward and forward movement than is usual in rodents, and strong jaw muscles. Loosened earth passed backward by feet, especially hind feet. Tunnels near surface but may be down to 2m (6ft) or more below ground. In very soft earth blunt head used to tamp excavated earth into wall of burrow instead of throwing it out to surface. Voice a squeak, sometimes a grunt, or explosive sound when alarmed. Preyed upon by Eagle owl (*Bubo bubo*) Long-eared owl (*Asio otus*) and Barn owl (*Tyto alba*).

Special features: where numerous, may be a pest to agriculture.

RUSSIAN OR GREATER MOLE RAT

ORDER	Rodentia
FAMILY	Spalacidae
GENUS	*Spalax*
SPECIES	*S. microphthalmus*

Description: like Lesser mole rat but larger, 242–310mm (10–12in) long and fur greyish with sandy tinge and white markings on head. Feeding and other habits, also habitat, as in Lesser mole rat. Range almost entirely confined to steppes of southern Russia.

SCRUB, BUSH OR WOODED STEPPES

Scrub forms a transitional zone between pure steppe and deciduous woodland, in which grasslands are broken here and there by areas of trees, typically oaks, with open grassy glades and scrub thickets around their perimeters. Most scrub at the present time represents a successional stage that will eventually change to woodland or back to grassland, but in some areas it is stabilized and represents the true climax vegetation.

Exposed coastal situations and sub-alpine areas above true forest as well as zones intermediate between steppe and woodland are all examples of temperate scrub.

Successional scrub communities are often very rich in plant species since they contain forms characteristic of grassland and also those characteristic of the margins of woodland. A good example of climax scrub occurs in the Burren of Western Ireland where, on limestone under the influence of heavy rainfall and strong winds, but in sufficient shelter to allow the growth of woody plants, extensive scrub is dominated by hazel, with an associated woodland flora; in more sheltered localities this merges into ashwood.

Where trees do establish themselves, one finds an accumulation of dead leaves on the ground surface. This leaf litter is responsible for two reasons for the more varied mammalian population found in scrub as opposed to pure steppe: it provides protection from extreme weather conditions for small mammals and it supports a diverse insect population that serves as a useful source of food.

Feeding relationships. Scrub and bush steppe display increased vegetational diversity which has led to a corresponding increase in the diversity and abundance of insect populations, with the emphasis shifted from the earthworm-dominated fauna. Thus insectivorous mammals come into their own. The most important species are the white-toothed shrews which compete successfully with insectivorous passerine birds and reptiles. Hedgehogs take larger insect prey and are more strictly nocturnal.

Availability of roosting sites coupled with denser flying insect populations allows some bats to establish themselves. However, the secondary carnivores now have several mammalian representatives,

mainly small mustelids, though in extreme southeastern steppes jackals may occur.

Herbivorous mammals show much reduced diversity from those in open steppe due primarily to less suitable terrain and competition from small passerines. It is interest-ing to note that both Hamsters and Birch mice take small birds (and mammals) to supplement their seed-eating habits.

Reliance on burrowing as is pre-dominant in open steppe is not evid-ent in the mammal populations. Denser cover renders it largely un-

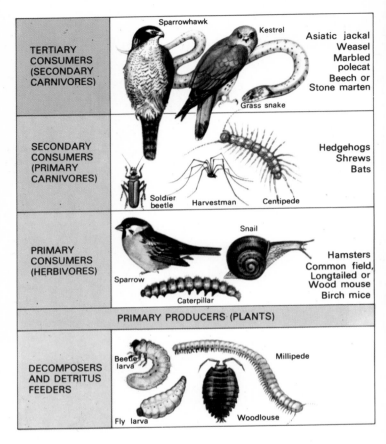

TERTIARY CONSUMERS (SECONDARY CARNIVORES)	Sparrowhawk, Kestrel, Grass snake	Asiatic jackal Weasel Marbled polecat Beech or Stone marten
SECONDARY CONSUMERS (PRIMARY CARNIVORES)	Soldier beetle, Harvestman, Centipede	Hedgehogs Shrews Bats
PRIMARY CONSUMERS (HERBIVORES)	Sparrow, Caterpillar, Snail	Hamsters Common field, Longtailed or Wood mouse Birch mice
PRIMARY PRODUCERS (PLANTS)		
DECOMPOSERS AND DETRITUS FEEDERS	Beetle larva, Fly larva, Woodlouse, Millipede	

necessary and independence from worm prey makes it unprofitable. Burrowing is therefore limited to a protective function as opposed to a mode of feeding and is shown to an appreciable extent only by Woodmice. True grazer-burrower herbivores are absent and the emphasis is towards the omnivorous habit in small mammals.

Hedgehog *Erinaceus europaeus.*

EUROPEAN HEDGEHOG

ORDER	Insectivora
FAMILY	Erinaceidae
GENUS	*Erinaceus*
SPECIES	*E. europaeus*

Description: back and top of head coated with sharply-pointed, dark-brown to black spines, 20mm (¾in) long, each set at an angle to skin. Rest of body clothed in coarse, brittle hair, yellowish-white to dirty brown. Occasional pale, rarely albino, individuals. No regular seasonal moult. Neck and body short in relation to bulk. Snout pointed, nose moist. Feet with 5 digits, all with strong claws. Front feet larger than hindfeet. Legs seem short and gait crouching but can move fast with body well clear of ground. Eyes black, fairly large. Gait usually hesitant. When moving swiftly has comical 'clockwork' action. Spines normally lie flat but are erectile. Rolls defensively into an almost complete ball of spines.

Male, head and body length: 188–263mm (8–10½in), tail 26mm (1in). Female slightly smaller. Weight varies considerably throughout year. Female weighs least in January at 800g (28oz) average, and reaches maximum in July at 1000g (35oz) average. Male averages 900g (31½oz) in June and reaches average maximum of 1200g

(42oz) in September or October. Maximum weights recorded: female 1355g (47½oz), male 1440g (50½oz).

Range: Eurasia (Ireland to Vladivostok), south of latitude 60°N to Mediterranean, including islands of Corsica, Sardinia, Sicily, Crete and Cyprus. Asia Minor and Transcaucasia.

Habitat: typically dry open land with scrub, bushes or shrubs; rare in dense woodlands. Up to 2600m (8000ft) above sea-level.

Life history: in courtship male trips, hissing and spitting, round female who pivots defensively. Breeding season May to July, with sometimes a second season, August or September. Gestation 30–40 days. 2–9 (average 7) blind, deaf and helpless young born in large nest of leaves in hedge-bottom or grass tussock, sparsely clad with pale flexible spines, with ears drooping. At birth 57–96mm (2¼–3¾in) long, weigh 8–25g (¼–⅔oz). 36–60 hours after birth second coat of spines appears between first spines. Lactation about 4 weeks. Eyes open 14 days. Males take no part in care of young. Female moves them to new nest if disturbed. Start to venture from nest at 3 weeks and forage following mother in single file. Weight doubled in 7 days, tenfold in 47 days, forty-fold in 98 days. Longevity 10 years, possible record of 14 years in captivity.

Feeding: typically searches leaf litter, bits of wood or stones, turning them over with snout. Sometimes digs with front paws. Omnivorous: insects, slugs, snails, earthworms, frogs and carrion. Sweet fruits, acorns and berries. Sometimes adders and slowworms, eggs. Sometimes drinks excessive amounts of milk or water. Some doubtful reports of attacks on poultry.

Habits: sleeps in nest in daytime not curled up but lying on front with head laid forward, resting on bedding material. Spines lie flat pointing backwards. Nest built of dry leaves, grasses and moss and placed in bottoms of hedgerows or in bramble thickets or burrows. Varies in size. Breeding nest large.

Normally silent but has many vocalisations. 'Snoring' towards evening when wakeful but not yet left sleeping nest, or if disturbed. Also snortings, snufflings, hisses. Ticking or clicking sound made with teeth. Young makes high-pitched whistle and a sort of quack or piping. Mother calling to young uses bird-like whistle. Loudest sound is scream, not a cry of pain but elicited mainly when hindleg held.

Almost entirely nocturnal, may be seen dusk to dawn. Sometimes suns

Hedgehog curled during hibernation.

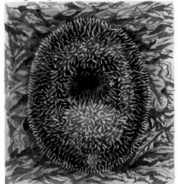

itself outside in daytime in warm weather. Hibernation starts mid-October but some individuals later, these sometimes seen foraging in December or January in frost or snow. Deepest sleep from January for several weeks. Then arousals become more and more frequent until Hedgehog awakens to full spring activity. Females survive hibernation better than males. Take fleas into hibernation. These do not hibernate but their breathing slows down.

Sight poor (partial colour vision), smell and hearing acute. Primitive brain, somewhat dim-witted, but can learn in captivity to respond to a name. Swims and climbs well.

Predators include Badgers, polecat, Tawny owl, sometimes magpies, Stoat and Weasel, Pine marten and Brown rat. Flooding in winter while hibernating is big hazard. Dogs and man disturb them during breeding season. Foot-and-mouth outbreaks in Hedgehogs (experimental work on foot-and-mouth disease carried out on Hedgehogs in laboratories).

Populations: little precise information (plentiful in gardens and parks in built-up areas). Many killed on roads. Early 1950's, estimated 1 per 0·4 hectare (1ac) in Great Britain. Germany in 1930's, estimated 1 per 11 hectares (25ac) acres. Numbers estimated to have fallen in 1960's in Great Britain in rural areas but still high in suburbs. Less persecuted now and many kept as pets.

ALGERIAN OR VAGRANT HEDGEHOG

ORDER	Insectivora
FAMILY	Erinaceidae
GENUS	*Erinaceus*
SPECIES	*E. algirus*

Description: slightly smaller than European hedgehog with more slender body, smaller hindfoot and head clearly marked from body. Ears broad and long. Underparts noticeably lighter than in European species and dark brown on flanks. Spines generally lighter in colour and those of head parted in middle.

Range: Mediterranean coast of Spain and France, Balearics; also Morocco to Libya and Canaries.

Habitat: similar to that of European hedgehog.

Habits: crepuscular mainly, walks higher on legs than European species. Does not hibernate.

Special features: whether this species, which is essentially North African, reached Europe by natural means or was introduced by man is still undecided. The French zoologist, Heim de Balsac, in 1936,

Algerian or Vagrant hedgehog *Erinaceus algirus*.

argued that it is a relict species, from the Pliocene. The sparse numbers found in the coastal strip of Spain and southern France, as well as its occurrence in the Balearics and Canaries, is the kind of distribution to be expected had it been taken as a pet from North Africa and become feral.

PYGMY SHREW

ORDER	Insectivora
FAMILY	Soricidae
GENUS	*Sorex*
SPECIES	*S. minutus*

Description: small delicately built body, long snout with long whiskers. Tail long and hairy usually exceeds $\frac{2}{3}$ of body length. Sandy brown above, underparts white with fairly sharp line of demarcation. Two moults, in spring and autumn. Albino and cream-coloured individuals recorded. Head and body length 53–63mm (2–2½in), tail 33–42mm (1¼–1½in), weight 2·4–5·6g ($\frac{1}{12}$–$\frac{1}{5}$oz).

Range: whole of Europe except for Mediterranean zone.

Habitat: rough grassland, heather moors, open woodland, mountain scree.

Pygmy shrew *Sorex minutus*.

Life history: breeding starts in April, reaches a peak in June and usually ends in August. Gestation probably 22 days. At least 2 litters a year with 2–8 young weighing 0·25g (1oz) at birth. Weaned about 22 days.

Feeding: probably similar to that of common shrew but little detailed information.

Habits: alternate periods of rest and activity throughout 24 hours with higher peaks of activity during day. Does not construct runs but uses runways of other animals. Moves very swiftly with very quick reactions. Climbs well. Nests, in clumps of rushes, hollow tree stump or hollow in ground, made of moss, dry grass, wood chips combined and interwoven into hollow ball. Main predators owls. Voice like common shrew, squeaks or screams in aggression, twitters when exploring.

SAVI'S PIGMY OR ETRUSCAN SHREW

ORDER	Insectivora
FAMILY	Soricidae
GENUS	*Suncus*
SPECIES	*S. etruscus*

Description: smallest known mammal, reddish grey-brown shading to dirty grey on underside. Long

hair scattered between normal hairs of coat and more numerous on tail. Teeth white. Ears larger and more

Savi's pygmy or Etruscan shrew
Suncus etruscus

conspicuous than is usual in shrews. Tail long in relation to body, blackish-brown above, lighter underneath. Head and body 36–52mm (1½–2in) long, tail 24–29mm (1in) weight 1·5–2g ($\frac{1}{20}$–$\frac{1}{15}$oz).

Range: Mediterranean region, including Iberian peninsula, southern France, Italy, Dalmatia, Greece and associated islands.

Habitat: arable land and gardens.

Feeding: presumably as in Common shrew but nothing known except for observations on captive individuals.

Life history: Nothing known.

Habits: rests in nests between tree roots and in cavities in stone walls.

BICOLOURED WHITE-TOOTHED SHREW

ORDER	Insectivora
FAMILY	Soricidae
GENUS	*Crocidura*
SPECIES	*C. leucodon*

Description: dark grey-brown above, paler, more yellowish-white underneath, with sharp demarcation between the two colours. Long silvery-grey hairs among normal hairs on flanks, rump and, particularly, tail, which is relatively short, grey-brown above, white underneath. Ears conspicuous and clear of body fur. Head and body 64–87mm (2½–3½in), tail 28–39mm (1–1½in), weight 6–15g ($\frac{1}{4}$–$\frac{1}{2}$oz).

Bicoloured white-toothed shrew *Crocidura leucodon* **with young in caravan formation.**

Range: from northwest France through central Europe to southeast Russia, from about latitude 52°N southwards reaching parts of western Italy and eastern Greece.

Habitat: on fringes of woods and elsewhere under shrubs and dense vegetation and in gardens. In eastern parts of range habitat is in steppe country.

Feeding: similar to Common shrew.

Life history: similar to Common shrew, young weaned at 3 weeks, sexually mature in year of birth.

Habits: active by day and night but more so at night. Makes nest of fresh or dry grass. Voice a shrill cry, also a high-pitched twittering and a soft humming long drawn out.

Lesser white-toothed
or Scilly shrew
Crocidura suaveolens

LESSER WHITE-TOOTHED OR SCILLY SHREW

ORDER	Insectivora
FAMILY	Soricidae
GENUS	*Crocidura*
SPECIES	*C. suaveolens*

Description: similar to Bicoloured white-toothed shrew but smaller, with more variable colour, grey to brown or red, of upperparts, underparts ochreous yellow and tail only indistinctly bi-coloured. Also, tail bears numerous long bristles which project beyond ordinary hairs, ears prominent giving fox-like face. Head and body 53—82mm (2—3¼in), tail 24—44mm (1—1¾in), weight 3·5g (⅛oz). Occupying similar habitat to *C. leucodon* but more southerly, and with isolated communities on the Isles of Scilly, Jersey and Sark in the Channel Islands, and a few islands off the west coast of France. Life history, habits and ecology little known.

COMMON EUROPEAN WHITE-TOOTHED SHREW

ORDER	Insectivora
FAMILY	Soricidae
GENUS	*Crocidura*
SPECIES	*C. russula*

Description: similar to Bicoloured shrew and only slightly larger. Races on some Mediterranean islands larger with relatively longer tails.

White-toothed shrew *Crocidura russula*.

Upperparts lighter and more reddish than in Bicoloured shrew, underparts yellowish-grey and not sharply demarcated from upperparts, tail indistinctly bicoloured.

Range: Continental Europe from Holland to Gibraltar eastwards to Poland, Hungary, Yugoslavia and Greece, south to Mediterranean, including islands. Also Israel and North Africa.

Habitat: dry meadows, hedges, gardens to fringes of woods.

Feeding: similar to Common shrew.

Life history: breeds in year of birth. Caravanning by young observed in this and other species of *Crocidura,* in which each holds tail of one in front near base, in its mouth, the mother leading. All move in step.

Habits: mainly nocturnal; prey of owls, especially Barn owl *Tyto alba.*

Schreiber's bat *Miniopterus schreibersii*.

SCHREIBER'S BAT

ORDER	Chiroptera
FAMILY	Vespertilionidae
GENUS	*Miniopterus*
SPECIES	*M. schreibersii*

Description: medium-sized, greyish-brown above, paler underparts, tail and hindlegs long, feet small, tail completely enclosed in interfemoral membrane. Domed head. Wings broad at base, pointed at tips. Ears short, truncated, tragus long, slender. Head and body length 52–60mm (2–2½in), tail of similar length, weight 8–11g ($\frac{1}{3}$–$\frac{2}{5}$oz).

Range: southern Europe, south of latitude 48°N, including Mediterranean region and most islands.

Habitat: away from human settlements; hibernates in caves but may occupy large isolated buildings winter and summer.

Habits: emerges early, flies high and fast; partially migratory.

GREY OR MIGRATORY HAMSTER

ORDER	Rodentia
FAMILY	Cricetidae
GENUS	*Cricetulus*
SPECIES	*C. migratorius*

Description: vole-like but with large eyes and ears and short tail. Upperparts light reddish-brown, underparts white. Head and body 87–117mm (3¼–4¾in), tail 22–28mm (1–1¼in), weight 33–38g (1–1⅓oz).

Range: central Asia species extending to Ukraine with isolated populations in Bulgaria and Greece.

Habitat: steep wooded slopes in forest-steppe; also cultivated land.

Life history: 2–3 litters a year of 5–6 young.

Feeding: eats seeds, leaves, buds, insects, also stores these in burrows.

Habits: nocturnal, burrowing with 1–5 tunnels leading to a nest lined with leaves and leaf-stems, at depths of 62–124cm (2–4ft). Authorities disagree on whether it hibernates or not. Prey of fox, Stoat, Marbled polecat.

COMMON FIELD, LONG-TAILED FIELD OR WOOD MOUSE

ORDER	Rodentia
FAMILY	Muridae
GENUS	*Apodemus*
SPECIES	*A. sylvaticus*

Description: dark yellow-brown fur on upperparts, underparts white; line of demarcation distinct. Spot of buff or orange on chest. Long snout.

Dark eyes prominent, long oval ears have inner margin turned inwards at base. Long tail dark brown above, whitish below. Juveniles have much

Wood or Long-tailed field mouse
Apodemus sylvaticus.

greyer coats. Silver-grey and melanic forms recorded. Moults mainly in spring and autumn. Females slightly larger than males. Head and body length: 81–94mm ($3\frac{1}{4}$–$3\frac{3}{4}$in), tail 76–100mm (3–4in), weight 14–29g ($\frac{1}{2}$–$\frac{3}{4}$oz).

Range: Europe as far north as Sweden and Norway, eastwards across central Asia to Pacific. North Africa.

Habitat: woodlands, fields, hedgerows, gardens. Will occasionally occupy houses and buildings in winter, especially where no house mice present.

Life history: breeding occurs throughout summer in north of range, throughout year farther south. Gestation 25–26 days. Several litters a year each with 2–9 (usually 4–6) young born naked and blind. If female alarmed, will run with half-grown babies hanging to her teats and keeping in step. Young weaned at 21 days and, except for those in late litters, start to breed same year. Longevity 2 years but mean expectancy only about 6 months.

Feeding: omnivorous: acorns, nuts, haws, grain and smaller seeds, fruits, buds, green plants, bulbs, fungi. Also insects, insect larvae, spiders. Food stored, especially nuts and acorns, for winter use. Damage done to garden crops.

Habits: activity almost entirely nocturnal. Less active in winter but does not hibernate. Very quick in movements. When alarmed moves in zigzag. Bounds like miniature kangaroo, with leaps as high as 90cm (3ft), landing with all four feet together; agile climber. Uses runways in and under leaf litter. Swims well if necessary. Gregarious but female drives male from nest as soon as pregnant. When two mice meet, ritualised 'boxing' or sniffing noses ensues. Burrows made underground may be extensive. Breeding nest a ball of dry grass usually built in separate chamber of burrow or under roots of tree. Winter food also stored in burrows. Special chambers in burrows for use as latrines. Voice a high squeaking but seldom heard. Preyed upon by owls, foxes, Weasels, Stoats, Hedgehogs, Vipers, Wild and feral cats.

NORTHERN BIRCH MOUSE

ORDER	Rodentia
FAMILY	Dipodidae
GENUS	*Sicista*
SPECIES	*S. betulina*

Description: mouse-like, with habits similar to Dormouse. Russet on back to white on flanks and underparts with a black stripe from top of head to base of prehensile tail. Long hindlegs. Snout blunt, eyes and ears moderately large. Tail $1\frac{1}{2}$ times length of head and body combined, which is 52–70mm (2–2$\frac{3}{4}$in) long, tail being 79–106mm (3–4in). Weight 6·5–13g ($\frac{1}{4}$–$\frac{1}{2}$oz).

Northern birch mouse *Sicista betulina*.

Special features: cairns of small stones or twigs sometimes built over or beside entrance to burrow but purpose unknown.

Range: discontinuous distribution over northern and eastern central Europe, south to Danube.

Habitat: birch copses, open parkland, oatfields; mainly in mountains in southern parts of range.

Feeding: food mainly insects living in rotten wood or under bark, some seeds taken.

Life history: breeds May to June. Gestation four weeks. One litter a year, usually 4–5 young born blind,

naked, helpless, growing relatively slowly and remaining in nest for 5 weeks. Eyes open at 25 days.

Habits: mainly crepuscular and nocturnal. Agile, climbs well using prehensile tail, runs rapidly often with tail held, straight or bent, upwards. Nest of moss in cavity of rotting tree trunk. Hibernates October to April when body temperature drops to 7 °C.

Southern birch mouse *Sicista subtilis.*

SOUTHERN BIRCH MOUSE

ORDER	Rodentia
FAMILY	Dipodidae
GENUS	*Sicista*
SPECIES	*S. subtilis*

Description: similar to Northern birch mouse. Russet fur with black dorsal stripe, bordered either side with yellowish stripe, running from nose-tip to base of prehensile tail. Moderately long hindlegs. Head and body 55–68mm (2–2¾in) long, tail 67–82mm (2⅔–3¼in), weight 9·5–14g (⅓–½oz).

Range: steppe zone of southern Russia (and Asia), extending westwards to Rumania with isolated distribution in Hungary and Austria.

Habitat: typically densely grown steppes, open woodlands, arable land.

Habits: similar to Northern birch mouse but more nocturnal, hibernates in a nest of grass in cavities in trees, rocks or walls, or in ground, and uses storage chambers for food.

GOLDEN OR INDIAN JACKAL

ORDER	Carnivora
FAMILY	Canidae
GENUS	*Canis*
SPECIES	*C. aureus*

Description: like a long lean dog with large erect ears, long muzzle, long legs and bushy tail. Coat is dirty yellow with black and brown hairs. Tail reddish-brown, black-tipped. Head and body length 560–740mm (22–29in), tail 230–360mm (9–14in), height at shoulder 406mm (16in), weight 6·8–11kg (14–24lb).

Range: southeastern Europe, partly in Russia, partly in Balkans. Southern Asia. Central and North Africa.

Golden or Indian jackal *Canis aureus*.

Habitat: steppes with thickets or scrub vegetation, seldom in woods. Often enter towns and cities.

Life history: mating season January or February. Gestation 60–70 days. Usually 4–5 young born in April. Both male and female parents feed young. Begin to forage for themselves at 8 months but are not independent until 10 months.

Feeding: scavengers and carrion eaters but also hunters. Serious raider of poultry, occasionally taking domestic sheep or goats. Any food

Food of the jackal: (1) rabbits, (2) small mammals, (3) reptiles, (4) birds and (5) invertebrates.

not eaten is buried to be consumed later. Food: small mammals, birds, eggs, fish, insects, fruit, carrion, household scraps.

Habits: lives in pairs or small family groups. Hunts mostly at dusk and at night. Pairs hold territories marked with urine by both sexes. Territorial disputes usually settled by aggressive displays. Young born in burrow dug by mother or in enlarged fox or badger holes.

Voice a high-pitched whine used for communication.

Footprint of the jackal.

Heavily persecuted by man especially in populated areas because of its raids on poultry and domestic animals.

WEASEL

ORDER	Carnivora
FAMILY	Mustelidae
GENUS	*Mustela*
SPECIES	*M. nivalis*

Description: smallest species of Carnivora. Reddish-brown upperparts, white underparts. Often spots and blotches of dark colour on underparts. Short, uniformly coloured tail. Long slender body, short limbs, long neck and small head giving snake-like appearance when moving. Upright, rounded ears. Probably two moults a year. In north of range turns white in winter. Young have greyer and duller back and

Weasel *Mustela nivalis.*

more creamy underparts. Glands under tail secrete musk. Measurements highly variable: average male head and body length 200mm (8$\frac{1}{2}$in), average length of tail 60mm (2$\frac{3}{4}$in). Female 25mm (1in) or so less than male in length. Average weight of male 115g (4oz), female 59g (2oz). Formerly believed that Least weasel occurred in parts of Europe but this now generally agreed to be a subspecies of *Mustela nivalis.*

Range: Europe, across Asia to Japan and from Siberia in north, southwards into China and Afghanistan. North Africa. Least weasel in North America now generally agreed

to be a subspecies of *Mustela nivalis.*

Habitat: almost every type of habitat including woods, scrubland, hedgerows, rocky country, barns and even large towns.

Life history: breeding March to August. Gestation about 6 weeks. Usually 2 litters a year of 3–8, usually 5, young, weaned at 4 to 5 weeks and taught to hunt and kill by mother. Some young of first litter may breed in same year.

Feeding: hunts mainly at night alone, in pairs or in family parties. Stalks or trails prey and kills by bite at back of head. R* lentless killer and will attack animals much larger than itself. 'Charming' sometimes used. Some damage to poultry. Voles and mice principal food, also rats, moles, young Rabbits, frogs, small birds, eggs, occasional fish. Will pursue voles and mice in their underground runs. Occasionally will eat freshly killed shrews and very rarely carrion.

Habits: mainly nocturnal but sometimes active by day. Possibly has alternating spells of activity with periods of rest. Breeding nest of dry leaves, grass or moss in hole in bank or low down in hollow tree. In colder part of range winter den sometimes lined with fur of prey. No hibernation. Good climber and swimmer. Usual gait bounding. Courageous and ferocious out of all proportion to size. Territories marked with musk from anal glands, also released when disturbed and probably helps bring sexes together in breeding season. Hunts mainly by scent.

Voice a guttural hiss when alarmed and short screaming bark when disturbed. Neither heard very often. Young have shrill scream.

Man once most important enemy but now realised Weasel does more good than harm. Natural enemies: larger hawks, owls, foxes, Wild and domestic cats, sometimes Stoats. Incidence of nematode parasite very high.

Populations: numbers fluctuate with abundance of voles.

MARBLED POLECAT

ORDER	Carnivora
FAMILY	Mustelidae
GENUS	*Vormela*
SPECIES	*V. peregusna*

Description: resembles Common polecat (p. 114) in form but smaller and differs in colour of pelage, which

Marbled polecat
Vormela peregusna.

is mottled dark brown and cream with uniform dark brown underparts. Head and body 31—38cm (12—15in) long, tail 15—16·5cm (6—6½in) long.

Range: typically an inhabitant of Asiatic steppes and those of southern Russia, extending south-eastwards into coastal Rumania and into Bulgaria.

Habitat: open areas with scrub or trees, cultivated land and gardens. Sometimes seen on open steppes.

Habits: similar to those of common polecat but frequently sits erect on haunches or stands erect on hind-legs. Food similar, also, consisting of insects, lizards, small mammals and birds, especially quail.

BEECH OR STONE MARTEN

ORDER	Carnivora
FAMILY	Mustelidae
GENUS	*Martes*
SPECIES	*M. foina*

Description: similar to Pine marten (p. 153) in form but slightly heavier build, shorter legs, muzzle lighter in colour and throat patch white instead of yellowish and divided into left and right parts. Also, ears smaller and narrower and soles of feet not hairy, so pads are exposed. Head and body length 42—48cm (16½—18in), tail 23—26cm (9—10½in), height at shoulder 12cm (4½in), weight 1·3—2·3kg (3½—5½lb).

Range: most of Europe as far north as southern shores of Baltic, absent from British Isles and Mediterranean islands (present on Crete, race lacking white throat patch). Southwest Asia to Himalayas and Mongolia.

Habitat: typically rocky ground, less arboreal than Pine marten. Frequents neighbourhood of houses; enters towns.

Food of the Beech marten: (1) domestic fowl, (2) small mammals, (3) birds, (4) earthworms, (5) eggs and (6) fruit.

Habits: similar to those of Pine marten but prey in southern part of ranges includes more amphibians and reptiles than *Martes martes*. Voice used for variety of calls: chatters and growls when excited, hisses when violently excited and may even squeal.

Beech or Stone marten *Martes foina*.

HUMAN HABITATIONS

A number of animals make habitual or occasional use of human habitations and associated buildings and lands. In extreme cases these animals are said to be symbiotic or commensal with man. They include only a few mammals, some of which have been domesticated.

Urban or suburban environments, especially where sanitary conditions are primitive, provide rich sources of food and may also be attractive to some mammals because they do not harbour as many predatory species as are found in more 'natural' environments.

It is possible that domestic species such as the dog were at first colonizers of human habitations. One view put forward is that the dog's wild ancestor (presumably the Wolf) was drawn to the sites of human settlement by the opportunities for scavenging the middens. Whatever the truth may be, the dog found food and shelter, but how it became domesticated must remain a subject for speculation.

Apart from dogs, bats are commonly found in human habitations. When prehistoric man used caves as shelters he could almost be said to have become symbiotic with bats,

which used the caves as roosts and must have inhabited the caves first. As man built huts and later houses and other buildings, he was creating in effect artificial caves. Many bats hibernate in hollow trees or under loose bark, and both these niches are simulated in plenty in crude huts and, better still, in houses. So the bats have 'turned the tables' and become symbiotic on man. Basically, the bats gain shelter, but where farming is primitive (that is, not up to the best hygienic standards) stables and associated dung heaps encourage the presence of flying insects, giving some of the bats a feeding ground near the roost.

As well as the dog and the bats, an important symbiont in Europe is the House mouse. Little is known of its early history except that it was known to the Ancient Greeks. Modern research leaves little doubt that the House mouse originated in central Asia and spread from there across Europe, possibly as the result of a population explosion, aided no doubt in the first place by the human stores of cereal grain upon which the mice could feed. After that, the transition to eating other stored foods would have been easy.

Both the Black and the Brown rat also originated in central Asia and spread to Europe in a similar fashion. The Black rat reached the extreme west of Europe in the 12th century, the Brown rat in the 16th–17th centuries.

Shelter and readily available food has brought other mammals into houses. The Fat or Edible dormouse makes use of roof spaces and apple stores, as does also the Grey squirrel in Britain. The Yellow-necked mouse, by contrast, can enter houses in winter and either raid stored foods such as apples and nuts or, more usually, bring in nuts and hoard them in the house.

Feeding relationships. Animals that have succeeded in cohabiting with Man are opportunists. Their food resources are often concentrated but occur sporadically. They are also very varied. Reliance

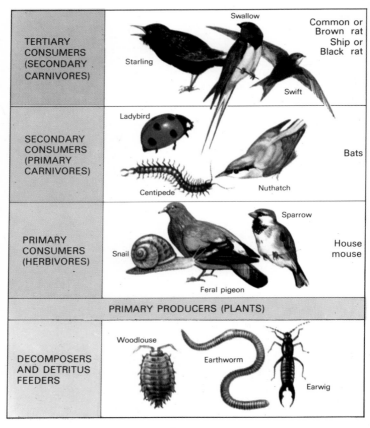

TERTIARY CONSUMERS (SECONDARY CARNIVORES)	Swallow / Starling / Swift	Common or Brown rat / Ship or Black rat
SECONDARY CONSUMERS (PRIMARY CARNIVORES)	Ladybird / Centipede / Nuthatch	Bats
PRIMARY CONSUMERS (HERBIVORES)	Snail / Feral pigeon / Sparrow	House mouse
PRIMARY PRODUCERS (PLANTS)		
DECOMPOSERS AND DETRITUS FEEDERS	Woodlouse / Earthworm / Earwig	

on decomposers and detritus feeders is less marked; earthworms and small insects appear in the diet of only a few predators, mainly passerine birds.

Most important among the primary consumers are House sparrows, Starlings and feral pigeons which partially overlap with rats and mice in selection of food items. The House mouse, Brown and Black rats are exceptions among mammals, having evolved an extremely adaptable behaviour repertoire and an omnivorous diet. Both have been key factors in their success in human habitations.

The House mouse is primarily herbivorous though will accept almost anything organic. Occasionally it takes insects, spiders, woodlice and detritus in outhouses.

The rats are still more catholic in their feeding habits and have been known to exist as carnivores. They may sometimes take small birds and mice, first neatly skinning the latter. Partly for this reason rats and House mice seldom cohabit.

BATS

The order Chiroptera, or bats, includes about 800 species, a little less than a quarter of the total species of mammals. The name means hand-winged, the bones of the fingers being enormously elongated with a membrane stretching between them which extends down the sides of the body to the hindlegs, forming a large and flexible wing. An interfemoral membrane stretches between the legs and usually encloses the tail. It is an extension of the membrane covering the limbs and functions as a steering vane and often as a temporary pouch for food. The flight muscles are anchored, as in birds, on a keel on the breastbone. The thumb is short, free of the wing and bears a claw, used in climbing. When resting, bats normally hang by the claws on the toes of the hindlimbs.

Bats fly in twilight or darkness, usually for relatively short periods and generally at dusk and again at dawn. Occasionally they migrate and banding has revealed that noctules may travel 2400km (1500mi). Both for navigating and hunting bats use an echo-location, or sonar, by emitting high frequency squeaks, above the range of human hearing, and receiving the echoes bounced back off solid objects. In most insect-eating bats these squeaks are given out through the open mouth but in horseshoe bats they are emitted through the nostrils which are sited at the middle of a horseshoe-shaped flap of skin on the face known as the noseleaf. The long-eared bat also uses the nostrils which are directed upwards, the sounds then being reflected forwards by the huge ears.

Bats in temperate regions mate in autumn. The spermatozoa received then by the females are stored in the womb until the spring, when a single ovum is produced and fertilized. The young are born in midsummer, the female hanging upright by her thumbs so that the single baby is prevented from falling by the pouch formed by the interfemoral membrane. It then climbs up through the mother's fur to a nipple in the armpit and holds firm to this with its milk teeth, protected by the mother's wing membrane. Nursing females sometimes carry their babies with them on foraging flights but more usually they leave them behind in the roost. During this period, from parturition until the young are independent, the females occupy a roost separate from the males. The young are suckled for several weeks before weaning.

The life expectancy is several years but banding has shown that individuals of some species may live nearly 30 years.

The order Chiroptera is divided into two suborders: the Megachiroptera and the Microchiroptera. The former, mainly larger than the Microchiroptera, are sometimes loosely referred to as 'the fruit bats' but although most are fruit-eaters, some are carnivorous, feeding on smaller bats. Others lap blood or nectar. The Microchiroptera are mainly insectivorous but some tropical species feed on nectar and pollen and closely resemble, in size as well as habits, those Megachiroptera with similar feeding habits.

As to European species of bats, the size of the insects taken by the various species varies roughly with the sizes of the bats. The larger bats take beetles, the smaller take flies or small moths. This is, however, a generalization, as is almost everything said, in the present state of our knowledge, about bats. It is, for example, possible to say that this or that species usually flies near the ground or at a height, or over water, but none of this serves as a reliable means of recognizing species. In fact, the only certain way of recognizing species, although a reasonable guess can often be made without, is to have the bat in the hand for identification.

Even then, careful measurements need to be taken to avoid confusing related species.

Bats are most numerous in the Tropics. The number of species encountered becomes fewer towards the colder regions, a not unexpected situation since insects (and fruit) are more abundant in regions where the temperature is higher. This is exemplified by the upwards of two dozen European species, which have their greatest concentration in southern Europe, with one species only, the northern bat, reaching the Arctic Circle.

NATTERER'S BAT

ORDER	Chiroptera
FAMILY	Vespertilionidae
GENUS	*Myotis*
SPECIES	*M. nattereri*

Description: head and body 50mm (2in), forearm 38mm (1½in), tail 38mm (1½in), wingspan 285mm (11¼in), weight 8–9·5g (¼oz). Ears oval, notched on outer margin, tragus long, slender, over half length of ear. Fur greyish-brown above, whitish on underside. Leaves roost early evening, hunts intermittently

throughout night. Europe except most of Scandinavia and Balkans.

Natterer's bat *Myotis nattereri*.

LARGE MOUSE-EARED BAT

ORDER	Chiroptera
FAMILY	Vespertilionidae
GENUS	*Myotis*
SPECIES	*M. myotis*

Description: head and body 63–91mm (2½–3½in), tail 45–60mm (1¾–2¼in), forearm 32mm (1¼in), wings broad, wingspan 350–450mm (14–18in). Ears large,

rounded, with 9–10 horizontal folds, tragus long, slender. Fur medium brown above, greyish-white below. Last joint of tail free of interfemoral membrane. Leaves roost late in

evening, flies slowly, straight, at moderate height, for 4–5 hours. Central and southern Europe, westwards to whole of France, southern and eastern England.

Large mouse-eared bat *Myotis myotis*.

LESSER MOUSE-EARED BAT

ORDER	Chiroptera
FAMILY	Vespertilionidae
GENUS	*Myotis*
SPECIES	*M. oxygnathus*

Description: very like Large mouse-eared bat but smaller (head and body never exceeds 74mm (3in)), ears more pointed and narrower, snout more pointed. Southern Europe.

LONG-EARED BAT

ORDER	Chiroptera
FAMILY	Vespertilionidae
GENUS	*Plecotus*
SPECIES	*P. auritus*

Description: head and body 50mm (2in), tail 34–50mm (1½–2in), forearm 38mm (1½in), wings broad, wingspan 250mm (10in). Ears long, transparent and marked with conspicuous transverse folds. Fur silky, brown on upper parts, paler below. Leaves roost half hour after sunset, flights intermittent throughout night, flies among trees 2·4–12·2m (8–40gt) from ground. All Europe except northern Scandinavia.

Long-eared bat *Plecotus auritus*.

GREY LONG-EARED BAT

ORDER	Chiroptera
FAMILY	Vespertilionidae
GENUS	*Plecotus*
SPECIES	*P. austriacus*

Description: very like Long-eared bat, distinguished by face being darker, sometimes almost black against the flesh-colour to light-brown of the commoner species and in being aggressive instead of docile. Central and southern Europe. Not certainly known from England.

Pipistrelle *Pipistrellus pipistrellus*.

Grey long-eared bat *Plecotus austriacus*.

COMMON PIPISTRELLE

ORDER	Chiroptera
FAMILY	Vespertilionidae
GENUS	*Pipistrellus*
SPECIES	*P. pipistrellus*

Description: head and body 38–50mm (1½–2in), tail 26–33mm (1–1⅓in), forearm 27–32mm (1–1¼in), wingspan 200–230mm (8–9in), weight 7·5g (¼oz). Ears short, broad, triangular with blunt tips, tragus small. Fur silky, dark to light reddish brown, paler on underparts. Leaves roost at dusk, flight rapid, jerky with much twisting and turning, at heights of 1·8–12·2m (6–40ft). Whole of Europe except northern Scandinavia.

NATHUSIUS' PIPISTRELLE

ORDER	Chiroptera
FAMILY	Vespertilionidae
GENUS	*Pipistrellus*
SPECIES	*P. nathusii*

Description: very like Common pipistrelle except that forearm 31–36mm (1⅕in) long, ears slightly larger and broader, thumb longer and colour lighter with more red. Eastern and east-central Europe with scattered distribution in western Europe.

Nathusius' pipistrelle *Pipistrellus nathusii*.

Kuhl's pipistrelle *Pipistrellus kuhli*.

KUHL'S PIPISTRELLE

ORDER	Chiroptera
FAMILY	Vespertilionidae
GENUS	*Pipistrellus*
SPECIES	*P. kuhli*

Description: very like Common pipistrelle but colour lighter, yellower, and distinct white margin to wing between last finger and foot. Mediterranean region, extending northwards to central France.

SEROTINE

ORDER	Chiroptera
FAMILY	Vespertilionidae
GENUS	*Eptisecus*
SPECIES	*E. serotinus*

Serotine *Eptisecus serotinus*.

Description: head and body 76mm (3in), tail 50mm (2in), forearm 50mm (2in), wings broad, wingspan 330—380mm (13—15in), weight up to 33g (1oz). Ear oval, tragus short. Fur dark brown with reddish tinge, lighter on underside. Leaves roost just after sunset, flies intermittently throughout night with heavy, fluttering, almost moth-like flight. Europe north to Baltic coast, England (south of line from Wash to Severn).

COMMON NOCTULE

ORDER	Chiroptera
FAMILY	Vespertilionidae
GENUS	*Nyctalus*
SPECIES	*N. noctula*

Description: head and body 82mm (3¼in), tail 41—59mm (1½—2⅓in), forearm 50mm (2in),

Common noctule *Nyctalus noctula*.

wings narrow, wingspan 350—380mm (14—15in), weight, unusually variable, 16—39g (½—1¼oz). Ears small, rounded, tragus small. Fur reddish-brown. Leaves roost just before sunset, or may be on wing as early as late afternoon. Quick dashing flight, similar to swifts with which it often hunts, 4·5—24·5m (15—80ft) high. Whole of Europe except most of Scandinavia, Scottish Highlands and Ireland.

EUROPEAN FREE-TAILED BAT

ORDER	Chiroptera
FAMILY	Vespertilionidae
GENUS	*Tadarida*
SPECIES	*T. teniotis*

Description: largest European bat with head and body up to 85mm (3½in) long and tail 46–57mm (2in) long of which a third to a half is free of interfemoral membrane. Flies high and fast. Mediterranean region.

European free-tailed bat *Tadarida teniotis*.

BLACK OR SHIP RAT

ORDER	Rodentia
FAMILY	Muridae
GENUS	*Rattus*
SPECIES	*R. rattus*

Description: 3 subspecies but probably only colour phases. *R.r. rattus*, pure black above, black or grey beneath; *R.r. alexandrinus*, brown above, grey beneath; *R.r. frugivorus*, brown above, white or cream beneath. More slender animal than brown rat with finer pelage.

Albinos recorded and white-spotting, especially on forehead and chest, not infrequent. Tail long, scaly, ringed, almost hairless. Snout projects far beyond short lower jaw; whiskers long and black. Ears naked. Feet pink with scale-like rings on undersides of digits and five pads on sole. Thumb of forefeet reduced to mere tubercle. Head and body length 165–228mm (6½–9in), tail up to

Subspecies of the Black or Ship rat *Rattus rattus*: (1) *R.r. alexandrinus* and (2) *R.r. frugivorus*.

Black or Ship rat *Rattus rattus*.

254mm (10in), weight variable, up to 200g ($\frac{1}{2}$lb).

Range: of Asiatic origin, migrated into Europe and carried from Middle Ages onwards all round world. Gradually giving way to Brown rat in more northern areas.

Habitat: in urban areas inhabits top stories of buildings, especially in seaports. Most common species of rat on ships. In rural areas often arboreal.

Life history: breeds throughout year with peak in summer and sometimes another in autumn. Gestation 21 days. Up to 5 litters a year, of 5–10 pink-skinned young born without fur, sight or hearing. Sexually mature at 3–4 months.

Feeding: stored cereal dominant food but anything that can be digested is eaten. Cannibalism may occur under unusual conditions.

Habits: mainly nocturnal. Range of movement rarely more than 90m (100yd). Very agile climber. Swims rarely. Although associated with garbage maintains own cleanliness spending much time cleaning fur and paws. In rural areas breeding nest made in trees. In urban areas roomy nest made of rags, paper, straw etc among rafters and behind partitions. Vocalizations include squeaks, squeals and screams. Preyed upon mainly by domestic cats in urban areas; in rural areas by various birds and beasts of prey.

Populations: decline in numbers in northern areas. Exterminated because of menace to stored foods and as carrier of bubonic plague. Not correct that Brown rat has driven out Black rat by agression in northern areas. More result of competition for food and living space.

Special features: hearing and smell acute. Myopic.

BROWN OR COMMON RAT

ORDER	Rodentia
FAMILY	Muridae
GENUS	*Rattus*
SPECIES	*R. norvegicus*

Description: fur on upper parts typically grey-brown with tawny tinge, more shaggy than that of black rat. Underparts dirty white. Stout body, tail short, thick scaly ringed, often bi-coloured, paler underneath. Ears covered with fine hairs. Feet flesh-coloured. Albinism, partial and total, and melanic forms occur. Albino form (white rat) used for laboratory research. Head and body length 203–267mm (8–10½in), tail 165–229mm (6½–9in), weight variable, up to 500g (1½lb).

Range: originated in central Asia, migrated into Europe, now worldwide in distribution. Predominates over black rat in temperate zones and almost completely supplants it in boreal and arctic regions.

Habitat: more terrestrial than Black rat and often forms extensive burrows. Occurs wherever man is, in warehouses, sewers, rubbish dumps, farm buildings, corn ricks. Also cultivated land, woodlands, river banks, rocky seashores.

Life history: breeds throughout year with one or two peaks. Gestation 24 days. 3 to 5 litters a year each of 4–10 blind, deaf, naked young but records of much larger litters. Female will defend young ferociously. Young leave nest at 3 weeks. Sexually mature 3 months.

Feeding: originally a grain-eater, has become omnivorous and a scavenger. Dominant food, stored cereal. Greenstuffs, animal food, stored root crops, meat in frozen meat stores also eaten. Shore-living rats feed on littoral molluscs, crustaceans and carrion. Insects in summer. Eggs: pest in chicken runs. Often more food is polluted than eaten. Stores food to some extent.

Brown or Common rat *Rattus norvegicus.*

Habits: Basically nocturnal with peak at dusk and before dawn. Good swimmer and diver and active burrower. Jumps well. Runways through vegetation and up sides of ricks obvious. Does not climb as well as Black rat. Successful and versatile species and very destructive. Cautious, avoids new objects in environment. Trap- and bait-shy. Vocalizations include squeals, squeaks and growls.

Predators in country: Stoat, Weasel, fox, polecats, owls. In urban areas: man, dogs and cats.

Track or runway left by Brown rat.

Populations: vary with habitat. Fertility so great and recovery so rapid that persecution by man quickly made good. When population reaches saturation, high mortality of young sometimes at rate of 99 % per annum. Stories of mass migration of rats moving in formation.

Special features: hearing and smell acute. Myopic. Known to carry away foods, including eggs, by trundling them along ground or held between forelegs. Two rats combining to transport an egg often reported, never scientifically confirmed.

HOUSE MOUSE

ORDER	Rodentia
FAMILY	Muridae
GENUS	*Mus*
SPECIES	*M. musculus*

Description: soft, brownish-grey fur, only little paler on underparts. Snout pointed; bright black eyes; large, sensitive brownish ears nearly half length of head; tapering, flexible and sparsely haired, scale-ringed tail. Distinctive musky smell. Considerable variations in colour, both darker and lighter than normal. Dark, nearly black and spotted variations. Domestic white mouse, an albino with pure white fur, pink eyes, feet and tail. Several cases recorded of mice hairless except for a few whiskers. Mice living permanently in meat refrigerators, larger and heavier with longer coats. Outdoor forms shorter-tailed, lighter-bellied. Size varies according to habitat, outdoor forms usually smaller with shorter tail. Larger, up to 102mm (4in) on outlying islands. Head and body length 70–92mm ($2\frac{3}{4}$–$3\frac{1}{2}$in) with tail about same length. Weight 10–41g ($\frac{1}{4}$–$1\frac{1}{3}$oz).

Range: probably originated in central Asia, has spread, or been accidentally transported, to every inhabited part of the world.

Habitat: town buildings, food

House mouse *Mus musculus* in brown, grey and albino varieties.

stores, farm premises especially in corn ricks; coal mines, open fields, particularly arable, woods, sand dunes, hedgerows. Large meat stores.

Life history: breeding occurs throughout year but reduced in winter in field-living populations. Gestation 19–20 days. Up to 10 litters per year in corn ricks, about 8 in grain stores, 6 in cold stores, 5 in houses; usually 5–6 young in litter, born blind and naked. Weaned at 18 days. Begin to breed at 6 weeks. Longevity up to 3 years, 6 years in captivity.

Feeding: basically seed and grain eaters, readily adapting to wide variety of other foods. Need very little water. Those living on household wastes seem unable to revert to natural foods (St Kilda mice died out when human occupants went). Food: seeds, grain, household wastes, flour, meat (in cold stores).

Habits: mainly nocturnal, but not completely so. Considerable individual variation in daytime activity. Breeding nests made from any available material, eg grass, shredded newspaper. Where stored grain plentiful may have communal nests. In cold meat stores nests made in carcases. Moves quickly and silently. Climbs well up walls of brick or concrete. When alarmed will leap surprising distances. Can squeeze through hole as small as 10mm ($\frac{3}{8}$in). Territories marked with urine and defended vigorously. Social structure loose until population becomes dense, then social hierarchy formed with one male dominant over the rest and he alone mates with the females.

Vocalizations, a well-known squeak. 'Singing' mice with diseased larynx or lungs. Use ultrasonics, babies to call mother, adults to communicate with each other or even as form of echo-location for finding way in dark.

In towns and on farms enemies mainly man and domestic cats. Many mammals and birds, especially feral cats and owls, as well as snakes, prey on wild-living individuals.

Populations: density in ricks very high and in houses where food plentiful. Mass increase to plague proportions especially in areas to which introduced, eg Australia, United States. Rate of infestation in London in recent years one building in every 100. Success due to high breeding rate and adaptability in finding food and shelter.

Senses: senses of smell and hearing two most important. Ears will follow course of moving object, suggesting they are highly sensitive to vibrations in air. Can pick up ultrasonic sounds. Sight poor, doubtful whether they see much beyond range of 50mm (2in). Sight in dark not fully studied.

BROADLEAVED WOODLANDS

Broadleaved woods and forests are dominated by deciduous trees although they do contain some that fail to shed their leaves in autumn. They are found north of the Mediterranean zone, where the Gulf Stream causes winter rains to be replaced by evenly distributed rainfall or rain with a summer maximum, and where the cold season is relatively short. They range east to the Urals as a wedge between the steppes and the boreal coniferous forests.

Deciduous trees occur where there are four to six months with adequate rain and they are absent from extreme maritime climates of the western seaboard as well as from regions with an extreme continental climate.

Broadleaved forests once covered most of Western Europe, but the climatic conditions that favour their growth also favour prosperous agriculture and grazing, and the broadleaved forest zone of Europe is now one of the most populous regions of the world. As a result only tiny fragments of the forest remain, with virtually none in virgin condition. In England, for example, many woods are situated on the site of primeval forest (as shown by the diversity of their tree species), and there has been continuous forest cover since the last Ice Age. However, their structure and the numbers of different species are strongly influenced by many centuries of silviculture.

Many authors recognize three layers of vegetation in broadleaved woodlands: trees, woody shrubs and herbaceous plants. Others prefer to subdivide the vegetation into five layers: trees over 5m (15ft), trees and shrubs under 5m, scrub undergrowth, a ground layer of grasses and herbaceous plants and a layer composed of mosses, lichens and fungi. Beech, oak, lime and ash are locally dominant in the tree layer, and in wet places alder and willow become common. The shrub layer is commonly composed of hazel, field maple and hawthorn. The trees flower early, commonly before the leaves open, and most are wind-pollinated; this allows a long period for fruits to form and ripen before the onset of winter. In early spring before the canopy becomes leafy the forest floor herbs flower, and the carpets of blossom, especially of bluebell, primose or oxlip, are one of the glories of broadleaved wood-

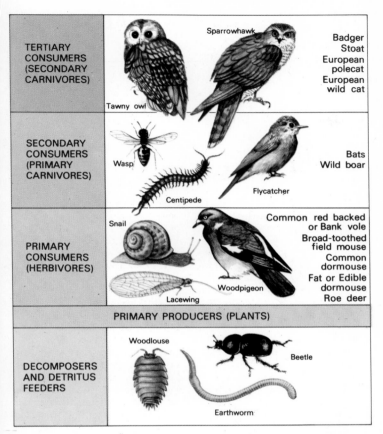

TERTIARY CONSUMERS (SECONDARY CARNIVORES)	Sparrowhawk Tawny owl	Badger Stoat European polecat European wild cat
SECONDARY CONSUMERS (PRIMARY CARNIVORES)	Wasp Centipede Flycatcher	Bats Wild boar
PRIMARY CONSUMERS (HERBIVORES)	Snail Lacewing Woodpigeon	Common red backed or Bank vole Broad-toothed field mouse Common dormouse Fat or Edible dormouse Roe deer
PRIMARY PRODUCERS (PLANTS)		
DECOMPOSERS AND DETRITUS FEEDERS	Woodlouse Beetle Earthworm	

lands, equalled only by the spectacular yellow, orange and red tints of the dying foliage in autumn. During late spring these flowers are replaced by other herbs, such as wood sorrel.

The exact composition of broad-leaved woodlands is largely determined by the nature of the soil. Where the soil is chalky, beech are the dominant trees. They form a dense canopy of green in summer which allows only a little sunlight to penetrate. In consequence her-baceous plants do not thrive and the brown carpet of leaf litter is bare of greenery for most of the year.

Where the soil is heavier and composed of clay, for example, a more varied flora is able to establish itself and the layers just described are more apparent. In oak forest, as well as trees of between 6 and 27m (20–90ft), there are saplings and young trees and also shrubs, bushes and herbaceous plants, briars and brambles and climbing plants growing up into the vegetation above,

including ivy, honeysuckle and clematis. Some of the smaller trees are noteworthy as fruitbearers. On the ground are found ferns, mosses, bilberry, gorse and heather and many kinds of small flowering plants.

Feeding relationships. The yearly cycle of vegetational growth in broadleaved woodlands leads to a build-up of a leaf litter layer which supports a vast array of invertebrate life, particularly insects and worms, which form the basis of the bird food chains.

Passerine birds dominate woodland in general, and broadleaved woodland in particular, and are the chief competitors of mammals. Common and Edible dormice and Wood mice are predominantly fungivorous and suffer heavy com-

petition from the numerous finch and bunting species. The mice, however, supplement their diets with vegetable matter.

The wide diversity of insectivorous birds, particularly warblers, wrens and tits, monopolize the insect food supplies. Bats have become successful by adapting to the nocturnal habit so they do not compete with the day-feeding birds.

The Wild boar is essentially an omnivore but can be included as a primary carnivore on the basis of its predilection for beetles.

The secondary carnivore niches are filled, once again, mainly by birds: some passerines, but owls and hawks are the dominant forms. Successful mammals in this category have been the Badger, Stoat, polecats and the wild cat.

GREATER HORSESHOE BAT

ORDER	Chiroptera
FAMILY	Rhinolophidae
GENUS	*Rhinolophus*
SPECIES	*R. ferrum-equinum*

Description: head and body 70mm (2¾in), tail 32mm (1¼in). forearm 51mm (2in), wingspan up to 380mm (15in), weight varies throughout year, maximum in December, male 23·4g (¾oz), female 27·3g (⅘oz). Nose-leaf horseshoe-shaped. Wings broad. Ears large broad, with sharp recurved tip. Fur thick, woolly, ash-grey above, pale buff on underside, sometimes with pink or yellow tinge. Leaves roost in early evening, flies at intervals during night, usually low from few inches to 60–90cm (2–3ft), at most 3m (10ft), from ground. Central and southern Europe, southern England, South Wales.

Greater horseshoe bat *Rhinolophus ferrum-equinum*, showing the nose-leaf in side view.

LESSER HORSESHOE BAT

ORDER	Chiroptera
FAMILY	Rhinolophidae
GENUS	*Rhinolophus*
SPECIES	*R. hipposideros*

Description: head and body 63mm (2½in), tail 30mm (1⅕in), forearm 39mm (1½in), wingspan up to 220mm (9½in), weight up to 6g (⅕oz). Colour as in Greater horseshoe bat but without pink or yellow tinge and fur longer and more silky. Habits as in larger species but flight usually between 1·5–4·5m (4–15ft). Central and southern Europe, southern England, Midlands, Wales, western Ireland.

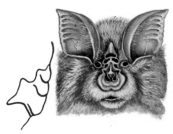

Lesser horseshoe bat *Rhinolophus hipposideros*, showing the nose-leaf in side view.

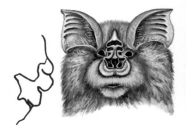

Mehely's horseshoe bat *Rhinolophus mehelyi*, showing the nose-leaf in side view.

MEDITERRANEAN HORSESHOE BAT

ORDER	Chiroptera
FAMILY	Rhinolophidae
GENUS	*Rhinolophus*
SPECIES	*R. euryale*

Description: intermediate in size between Greater and Lesser horseshoe bats, head and body up to 58mm (2⅕in), fur with lilac hue above, cream-coloured below and upper part of noseleaf more pointed. Southern Europe (in France, north to River Somme).

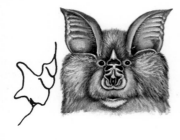

Mediterranean horseshoe bat *Rhinolophus euryale*, showing the nose-leaf in side view.

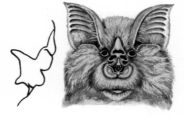

Blasius' horseshoe bat *Rhinolophus blasii*, showing the nose-leaf in side view.

BLASIUS' HORSESHOE BAT

ORDER	Chiroptera
FAMILY	Rhinolophidae
GENUS	*Rhinolophus*
SPECIES	*R. blasii*

Description: differs from other European horseshoe bats mainly in details of nose-leaf, colour of fur and head and body length as in Mediterranean horseshoe bat. Italy, the Balkans.

MEHELY'S HORSESHOE BAT

ORDER	Chiroptera
FAMILY	Rhinolophidae
GENUS	*Rhinolophus*
SPECIES	*R. mehelyi*

Description: differs from other European horseshoe bats mainly in details of nose-leaf. Size similar to that of Greater horseshoe bat, colour of fur as in Mediterranean horseshoe bat but paler. Discontinuous distribution in southern Europe, central France.

WHISKERED BAT

ORDER	Chiroptera
FAMILY	Vespertilionidae
GENUS	*Myotis*
SPECIES	*M. mystacinus*

Description: head and body 50mm (2in), tail similar, forearm

Whiskered bat *Myotis mystacinus*.

32–37mm (1½in), wingspan 240mm (9½in), weight 4·5–6g (⅙oz). Wings narrow. Ears long, slender, notched on outer margin with 4–6 transverse folds. Tragus straight, tapering, half length of pinna. Leaves roost early evening, hunts intermittently throughout night, usually picking insects off leaves, at 1·2–3·9m (4–13ft) from ground. Whole of Europe except extreme north and southern Iberia.

GEOFFROY'S BAT

ORDER	Chiroptera
FAMILY	Vespertilionidae
GENUS	*Myotis*
SPECIES	*M. emarginatus*

Description: similar in appearance and habits to Whiskered bat (above) but leaves roost later, has 6–8 transverse folds in ear and fur reddish. France to the Balkans, with a small area in central Portugal.

Geoffroy's bat *Myotis emarginatus*.

BECHSTEIN'S BAT

ORDER	Chiroptera
FAMILY	Vespertilionidae
GENUS	*Myotis*
SPECIES	*M. bechsteini*

Description: head and body 50mm (2in), tail 38mm (1½in), forearm nearly 44mm (1¾in), wingspan 250mm (10in), weight 9–11g (⅓oz). Ears large, oval, tragus long, slender.

Bechstein's bat *Myotis bechsteini*.

Fur soft, woolly, greyish-brown above, buff-grey below. Last joint of tail free of interfemoral membrane. Leaves roost late in evening, flies slowly at 1·5—5·2m (5—17ft). Low-lands of western to central Europe, from northern Iberia and France to western Russia with scattered areas outside including southern Britain and Midlands.

BARBASTELLE

ORDER	Chiroptera
FAMILY	Vespertilionidae
GENUS	*Barbastella*
SPECIES	*B. barbastellus*

Description: head and body 50mm (2in), tail 44mm (1¾in), forearm 38mm (1½in), wings narrow,

Barbastelle *Barbastella barbastellus*.

wingspan 330mm (13in), weight 6—8g (¼oz). Ears large, broad, united at bases above and below eyes so that eyes appear to be inside ears. Fur grizzled dark brown to almost black above, paler below. Leaves roost early in evening, flies with slow, flapping flight 4·6m (15ft) or less from ground. Central Europe extending in places into Mediterranean region, northwards to England, Wales and southern Scandinavia.

LESSER NOCTULE OR LEISLER'S BAT

ORDER	Chiroptera
FAMILY	Vespertilionidae
GENUS	*Nyctalus*
SPECIES	*N. leisleri*

Description: head and body 63mm (2½in), tail 38mm (1½in),

Leisler's bat *Nyctalus leisleri*.

forearm 44mm (1¾in), wings narrow, wingspan 250—300mm (10—12in), weight 14—20g (½—⅔oz). Similar to Noctule but smaller and fur darker. Leaves roost at or before sunset, one flight with sometimes a second flight before sunrise, at 4·5—24m (15—80ft), even up to 91m (300ft). Central and eastern Europe mainly with small areas over southern and western Europe and British Isles.

EDIBLE, FAT OR SQUIRREL-TAILED DORMOUSE

ORDER	Rodentia
FAMILY	Gliridae
GENUS	*Glis*
SPECIES	*G. glis*

Description: largest of European dormice and most squirrel-like. Fur grey-brown. Dark stripes on outsides of legs, dark ring round eyes. Pupil dark and horizontal. Long bushy tail. Head and body length 130–190mm (5–7½in), tail 110–150mm (4¼–6in). Weight 70–200g (2½–7oz).

Range: central and southern Europe, east to southwest Asia. Feral in small area in southern England.

Habitat: mature deciduous woodland, and especially in orchards. Sometimes conifer plantations. Frequently enters houses prior to hibernation.

Life history: in Europe breeds mid-June to August. Probably only one litter a year. 2–7 young (usually 4 or 5). Probably do not breed until after second winter. Longevity up to 6 years.

Feeding: mainly vegetarian with some insect food. Can be serious pest to fruit crops and to conifer plantations. Not known to store food. Food includes all kinds of fruit and nuts, seeds, bark of willow, plum and conifers, insects, less often birds' eggs and nestlings.

Habits: sleeps by day in summer in nest high in tree, in hole or fork close to trunk. Winter nest for hibernation may also be in hollow tree but frequently in cavity amongst roots of tree, or in thatch or lofts. Most active at night. Hibernates October to April. Prior to hibernation becomes very fat. May lose 35–50 % weight during hibernation. Enemies, dogs, cats, rats, Stoat, Weasel, owls, especially Tawny in Germany. Vocalizations include squeaks and snuffling, grunting, growling. When very fat considered edible and a favourite delicacy in ancient Rome. Very agile climber. May be noisy when in houses. Normally sedentary. Home range c. 100m (110yd). Autumn dispersal up to 1200m (¾mi).

Edible, Fat or Squirrel-tailed dormouse *Glis glis*.

Hazel dormouse
Muscardinus avellanarius.

COMMON OR
HAZEL DORMOUSE

ORDER	Rodentia
FAMILY	Gliridae
GENUS	*Muscardinus*
SPECIES	*M. avellanarius*

Description: fur of upper part light tawny, underside yellowish-white. Throat and adjoining part of chest purer white. Head comparatively large, blunt muzzle, prominent eyes, broadly rounded ears and long whiskers. Thickly furred tail. Forelimbs much shorter than hindlimbs with four separate fingers and rudimentary thumb. Hindfeet have five toes, one vestigial. All claws short and six large pads on underside of each foot. Unusual transverse ridges on molar teeth give rasping surface. Moult into winter pelage October. Spring moult – no information.

Hazel dormouse in hibernation.

Young greyer than adults, which vary between greyish and reddish. Form with white tip to tail not infrequent. Albinos recorded but rare. Average length about 139mm (5½in) of which nearly half is tail. Weight variable from 23–43g (¾–1½oz), greatest just before hibernation.

Range: Europe from France to Urals, no farther north than Sweden. Mainly in southern parts of British Isles. Asia Minor.

Habitat: copse, thick hedgerow, scrub and secondary growth in woods where trees have edible seeds, eg hazel and beech. Spends most of time above ground. Especially linked with honeysuckle; uses bark for nests.

Life history: Gestation c. 23 days. Usually 2 litters, late June to early July and late July to early August even into September and one record for October. Usually 3 or 4 in litter but may be up to 7. Female drives male away from nursery nest to a sleeping nest on his own nearby. Young born blind and naked. Furred in 13 days, moult at 18 days to adult fur but paler. Eyes open at 18 days, forage out of nest at 30 days and independent at 40 days. Sexually mature at about a year.

Feeding: mainly vegetarian, foraging above ground. Habit of sitting up on haunches and holding food in fore-paws, like squirrel. Does not crack shell of nut but gnaws small hole in it. Food: tree fruits including beech, hazel, chestnut, seeds of conifers, shoots and bark of trees, some insects especially in early summer. Has been said sometimes to take birds' eggs or even young birds.

Habits: strictly nocturnal but juveniles occasionally out by day. Sleeps during day in globular nest made of twigs, honeysuckle bark, moss and grass about 76mm (3in) in diameter, sometimes with round opening. Usually above ground suspended in bushes but may be among stubs of coppice or under tussock of grass. 3–5 nests made in a season. Always solitary in nest except in breeding season. Nests sometimes slightly colonial. Nursery nest twice size of sleeping nest, often made of honeysuckle bark shredded into ribbons, lined with finer materials and bed of leaves. Hibernation nest at or below ground level under moss at base of tree or in hedgebottom, under vegetable litter. Daily sleep approaches deep sleep of hibernation. Hibernation October to April. Always solitary, in own nest. Before hibernation accumulation of fat in body. (Some observers claim sleep not continuous but dormouse wakes at intervals for a meal from stored food). Dormouse rolls into ball for hibernation and can be rolled across table without giving sign of being disturbed.

Silent animal usually but soft chirping sound often heard. Soft hissing or whistling sounds when excited.

Relatively immune from predators while active but very vulnerable when hibernating; from magpies, Carrion crows, foxes, Badgers, Stoats, Weasels and rats. Estimated 4 out of 5 dormice killed during hibernation.

Populations: more rare than formerly in parts of range: the reasons for this are not clear. Very common in Czechoslovakia after good mast years and damages young trees seriously.

Bank vole *Clethrionomys glareolus*.

COMMON REDBACKED OR BANK VOLE

ORDER	Rodentia
FAMILY	Cricetidae
GENUS	*Clethrionomys*
SPECIES	*C. glareolus*

Description: fur of upper parts bright chestnut or vandyke brown, hairy tail black above, ending in pencil of hairs. Underparts including lower side of tail whitish varying to yellowish or buff. Moults can be seen at all times of year but peaks in spring and autumn. Black and albino varieties recorded. Pale, sandy mutant not uncommon. Island races usually darker in colour. Lips pink, feet grey, whiskers 25mm (1in) long. Ears and feet proportionately large, ears more oval than round. Sexes similar. Molar teeth rooted in jaw in adults, unlike other voles. Head and body length 88–101mm (3½–4in), tail variable 40–66mm (1½–2½in), weight variable 15g (½oz) in winter to double or more in summer.

Range: Europe, from Arctic Circle south to Mediterranean region, absent from most of Balkan and Iberian peninsulas.

Habitat: most abundant in deciduous woodland and scrub. In

111

Scandinavia often in conifer woods. Also banks, hedgerows. Likes well-developed scrub layer of bramble or bracken. Not common above tree-line but has been found in Scotland at 800m (2600ft) in bilberry growth. In northern latitudes, as in Norway, inhabits houses.

Life history: breeds usually April to October with peak in June. May be a small amount of winter breeding in southern parts of range. Males very quarrelsome; when fighting or pairing very vocal with grunting squeaks. Gestation c. 18 days. Litter size 3–6, several litters a year (possibly 4 or 5). Young born naked and blind c. 2g ($\frac{1}{25}$oz) weight. Weaned at $2\frac{1}{2}$ seeks. Sexually mature 4–5 weeks. First litters may produce second summer generation which reaches maturity following spring.

Feeding: vegetarian with small amount of animal food. Mostly taken on ground but in spring may climb rose and hawthorn bushes to nibble new leaves and in autumn hips and haws. Does not usually store food except in some northern regions. Fruits, seeds, especially cereals, nuts, berries, green herbage, roots, bulbs, fungi. Particularly fond of turnips. Insects and larvae, snails and even small birds and shrews also eaten. Also other Bank voles. In north eats shoot-buds of young conifers and gnaws bark.

Habits: active burrowers making runway system centred on nest at 20–100mm ($\frac{3}{4}$–4in) depth, used for sleeping at night. Breeding nest may be below or above ground (eg in bird's nest or tree stump), made of bark, grass and moss lined with softer material. Markedly diurnal when in thick cover but probably has normally alternating periods of activity and sleep throughout each 24 hours. Probably more active at night in summer. Does not hibernate.

Enemies, Tawny owl and Weasel especially but probably taken by most other predatory birds and mammals.

Not so noisy as Field voles but similar chattering and squeaking.

Special features: much more agile than Field vole but less given to jumping or burrowing. Good swimmer and diver. Good climber. Shallow runs in banks with many entrances and exits.

BROAD-TOOTHED FIELD MOUSE OR ROCK MOUSE

ORDER	Rodentia
FAMILY	Muridae
GENUS	*Apodemus*
SPECIES	*A. mystacinus*

Description: largest of field mice of genus *Apodemus*. Similar to Wood mouse (p. 74), but up to 150mm (6in) head and body, tail about same length. Range restricted to Greece, Albania and Dalmatian coast and Asia Minor. Sandy coloured with white underparts, it lives in open woods and thorn scrub, especially where ground is rocky. Almost nothing known of life history, habits and ecology.

Badger *Meles meles*.

BADGER

ORDER	Carnivora
FAMILY	Mustelidae
GENUS	*Meles*
SPECIES	*M. meles*

Description: rough coat appears uniform grey from distance but hairs are individually part black, part white, lighter portion nearest skin, then region of black, then white at tip. Hair colour varies widely. May be light areas from white through cream to sandy yellow or dark areas from black to reddish-brown; some silvery grey from old age, others very black coats, not true melanism as some white patches present. Albinos occasional. Single very long moult lasting most of summer. Undersurface and legs black. Head white with conspicuous black stripe either side running through eyes. Ears tiny tipped with white. Eyes small. Long tapering muzzle. Stout squat body. Short legs, 5 toes on each foot. Large powerful claws on front paws. Short tail. Badger immensely strong for size. Lower jaw hinged and cannot be dislocated without fracturing skull; accounts for Badger's tenacious grip. Prominent interparietal ridge in mid-line of skull. 750–930mm (2½–3ft) long. 300mm (1ft) at shoulder. Adult male 11·2kg (27lb); female, few pounds lighter. Some males up to 18kg (40lb). 3 records of 27kg (60lb) or over.

Range: practically all countries of Europe including some Mediterranean islands. Across northern Asia to southern China.

Habitat: set typically in woods or copses. Slopes preferred and old rabbit warrens often taken over. Also found on cliffs by sea, quarries, mountainsides, or under hedgerows, occasionally flat fields. Breeding sets up to altitudes of 500m (1700ft).

Life history: during mating season

good deal of play when scent of musk pronounced. Mating usually in July but may occur February to October. Cubs born January to May. Does not mean gestation of 7 months as there is delayed implantation. Embryo is only implanted in wall of uterus 7–8 weeks before actual birth and then development proceeds normally. Normal litter 2–3, may be 1–5. Usually one litter a year. Newborn cubs just under 120mm (5in) long, blind and dirty white in colour, no hair on undersides. Eyes open 10 days. At first head stripes faint but as hair becomes darker stripes on head more emphasized. Cubs remain below ground for 6–8 weeks after birth. When first emerge they keep close to mother and do not wander far. At 11 weeks cubs become more active, play more but still wary. Weaned 12 weeks or so. Remain with sow until autumn, sometimes throughout winter. Females (sows) sexually mature at 1 year-15 months; males (boars) at 1–2 years. Longevity more than 12 years.

Feeding: classified with Carnivora, having large canine teeth, but essentially omnivorous. Fairly wide diet dependent on availability: acorns, beech mast, wild fruits, oats, grass, clover, roots, beetles, night-flying moths, earthworms, slugs; also dig out nests of Bumble bees and wasps for grubs. Also take young Rabbits, lizards, mice, voles, amphibians, young birds fallen from nest, stillborn lambs, occasionally poultry. Have been known to maul carcases of deer and consume other carrion.

Habits: almost entirely crepuscular and nocturnal. Lives deep in earth, in a set, may be 3m (10ft) or more below surface; main entrance sloping down to passages and upper and lower galleries. Probably 'back door' some distance from main entrance. Mound of earth at main opening. Breeding chamber furnished with moss and grass used for birth of cubs. Sleeping chambers lined with heaps of bedding (bracken or grass) aired on sunny days. Hibernates in colder, more northerly parts of range, but winter sleep not very deep and, like bats, will emerge to feed if long thaw sets in. Elsewhere does not hibernate but is less active in winter. Can go 14 weeks without food, living on fat stored under skin.

Small cub makes high-pitched whickering, loud squeal when alarmed. Cubs playing make puppy-like noises. Adults growl or bark as a warning and purr with pleasure. Both boar and sow will scream, a long-drawn out eerie sound; reason not known.

Chief enemy man.

Special features: powerful digger. Keeps set clean, uses special latrines. Spring-cleans set in winter. Musk glands in anal region well developed, secrete musky liquid, emitted as a result of fear or excitement, setting scent trail or marking territory or used in mating season. Acute sense of smell. Ears and eyes both small, can hear well but sight not good.

Stoat *Mustela erminea*.

STOAT OR ERMINE

ORDER	Carnivora
FAMILY	Mustelidae
GENUS	*Mustela*
SPECIES	*M. erminea*

Description: upperparts reddish-brown, underparts white tinged with yellow. Tip of tail black. Demarcation line between upper- and underparts clearly defined. Lithe, long, slender body, short legs, upright rounded ears. In north of range fur in winter turns pure white except **Stoat in intermediate (1) and northern (2) winter fur.** for tip of tail remaining black (known as ermine). In intermediate zones, winter whitening is only partial. Secretion of musk from scent glands near base of tail. Spring and autumn moults. Head and body length 220–326mm (8½–12½in), tail 80–120mm (3–4¾in), weight (males) 200–440g (7oz–1lb), (females) 140–280g (5–10oz).

1

2

Range: eastwards across Europe from Great Britain, north to Arctic shores, south to Alps and Pyrenees. Into Asia across to Japan, south to Himalayas. In North America also called Short-tailed or Bonaparte weasel. Many subspecies described.

Habitat: typically woodland but most types of country included from fields, hedgerows and marsh to moorland and mountain.

Life history: fertile matings March, June, July, but implantation of embryos delayed until following spring. Gestation then 20—28 days. One litter a year April or May, 4 or 5 young, occasionally 6—9. Female alone tends young, defending them fiercely. Young covered with fine white hair at birth. Black tip appears on tail at 20 days. Eyes open 27 days. Weaning at 5 weeks. Remain with mother after weaning, hunting in family party, but female young soon become sexually mature and mate with older males.

Feeding: truly carnivorous, reject little that is flesh. Hunt mainly at night but sometimes by day. Prey largely pursued by scent. Hunts alone except after young are born when family parties may be seen. Hunts wherever there is food, keeping to cover. Kill made by bite at back of neck. Rabbits often paralysed at approach of Stoat. 'Charming' sometimes employed. Small rodents, such as mice and voles, main food. Rabbits, hares, rats, moles, fish, small birds, eggs, reptiles also eaten. Can be destructive to game and poultry.

Habits: usually sleeps by day. Den in hollow tree, rock crevice or burrow, used as focal point of home range. Nursery similar. Although mainly nocturnal often hunts by day.

Can swim and climb well. Moves in succession of low bounds. Alert, agile and energetic. Will play energetically together. Marked sense of curiosity. Smell and hearing acute. Sight poor.

Usually silent but when alarmed gives bark.

Persecuted by gamekeepers and poultry farmers. Few other enemies although some are taken by owls and hawks.

Populations: numbers may fluctuate widely, especially where prey species do same. May migrate in large numbers when prey scarce.

EUROPEAN POLECAT

ORDER	Carnivora
FAMILY	Mustelidae
GENUS	*Putorius*
SPECIES	*P. putorius*

Description: long coarse fur very dark brown on upperparts with dense yellowish underfur showing through. Underparts black. White or yellow patches between small ears and eyes and about muzzle. Short legs and bushy tail black. Long cylindrical body slung low with long neck. Anal glands with unpleasant smelling secretion. Considerable variation in colour; paler and redder forms. Female slightly smaller than

male and only a little over half the weight. Male, head and body length c. 410mm (16in), tail c. 180mm (7in), weight up to 2·05kg (4½lb).

Range: throughout Europe as far north as southern Sweden and southern Finland.

Food of the Polecat: (1) rats, (2) mice, (3) shrews, (4) moles, (5) fruit, (6) eggs, (7) birds, (8) amphibians, (9) domestic fowl, (10) reptiles and (11) beetles.

European polecat *Putorius putorius.*

Habitat: thickets, woods, scrub, sometimes close to human habitations.

Life history: mating in March or April. Gestation about 6 weeks. Probably only one litter a year with 3–8 (usually 5–6) young, blind and pure white: colours and markings appearing at about 3 months. May remain with mother until autumn.

A semi-domesticated Polecat, the ferret *P.p. furo,* is usually an albino form.

Feeding: mainly rats, mice and Rabbits. Will also take eggs, birds, fish, frogs, lizards and snakes. Heavily persecuted because of game and poultry killing.

Habits: solitary, nocturnal and terrestrial. Moves with gliding action (more like swimming than running). Den in any suitable hole such as fox earth or rock crevice. In winter may seek shelter in deserted buildings. Breeding nest made of dry grass. Hunts using keen sense of smell. Usually silent but sometimes yelps, clucks or chatters. Screams and hisses when frightened. Man the only important enemy. In former times was killed for pelt.

Steppe polecat *P.p. eversmanii.*

Wild cat *Felis silvestris*.

EUROPEAN WILD CAT

ORDER	Carnivora
FAMILY	Felidae
GENUS	*Felis*
SPECIES	*F. silvestris*

Description: stouter, longer body and longer limbs than normal domestic cat; squarish, robust head. Thick bushy tail with black rings and blunt black end. Fur generally long, soft and thick, yellowish-grey and always with black vertical stripes. Claws horn-coloured. Differs also from domestic cat in having high arch to nasal bones, larger carnassial teeth and very long gut. Average head and body length (male) 589mm (23in), tail 305mm (12in). Record of Scottish cat of 1·14m (3ft 9in) total length. Weight of average male

5kg (11lb) but may go up to 6·8kg (15lb), and one from Carpathians weighed nearly 15kg (33lb). Weight of female 3·8kg (8½lb).

Range: much of Europe and Africa and much of Asia to western China.

Habitat: thick woodlands and rocky mountainsides.

Life history: mating occurs usually in early March. Gestation 63 days. 2–4 kittens born early to mid-May (probably only one litter in truly wild

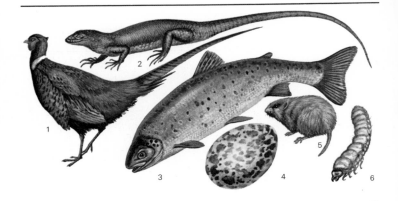

Food of the Wild cat: (1) birds, (2) reptiles, (3) fish, (4) eggs, (5) small mammals and (6) insect larvae.

cats. If second litter, in August, due probably to mixture of domestic strain). Leave nest 4–5 weeks, go hunting with mother 10–12 weeks, weaned about 4 months and leave mother 5 months. Sexual maturity year after birth.

Feeding: takes mostly small mammals, especially mice and shrews but also species up to size of hare and Rabbit, but may even kill Roe kid or well-grown lamb. Birds and occasionally fish and insects also eaten.

Habits: hunts alone or in pairs mainly at night with peaks of activity at dawn and dusk, by stealth and surprise rather than speed. Home range 60–70 hectares (150–175 acres). Territory marked by urine and by secretion from foot glands. Vision and hearing keen. Great strength and ferocity when hard pressed. Will climb but usually terrestrial. Den among rocks or in hollow tree. Voice a meeow, a growl when angry and a purr when pleased. Occasionally scream or caterwaul. Probably no serious enemies other than man. Hybridizes readily with feral domestic cat.

WILD BOAR

ORDER	Artiodactyla
FAMILY	Suidae
GENUS	*Sus*
SPECIES	*S. scrofa*

Description: large hog with bristly, pale grey to blackish hair, muzzle ending in mobile snout, canines curve outwards and upwards to project as defensive tusks, up to 30cm (1ft) long in male. Legs short, four hoofed toes on each foot, middle two used for walking. Head and body length up to 178cm (70in), tail up to 30cm (12in), weight of males

Wild boar *Sus scrofa*.

68–227kg (150–500lb), females 36–150kg (80–330lb). Sizes vary with locality, smaller and lighter in western and southern Europe, heavier and larger in eastern Europe.

Range: deciduous woodlands and Mediterranean zones of Europe and North Africa, through southern Asia to Malaya, Sumatra, Java, Philippines, Japan and Formosa. Introduced into many other countries, including United States.

Habitat: open deciduous woodlands.

Life history: rut November to February. Gestation 4 months, young

Wild boar with young.

121

usually born from March to May (in parts of Mediterranean basin breeding April to May). Large litters of up to 12 piglets, with bold longitudinal stripes of chestnut and yellowish-brown, able to run soon after birth and follow mother after few days. Probably two litters a year with sexual maturity at 2 years.

Feeding: greater part of diet vegetable: roots, bulbs, tubers, acorns, beechmast, but also rodents, young Rabbits, worms, snails and even reptiles and birds' eggs. Can be pest in cultivated areas by feeding on grain, potatoes, beet and by raiding vineyards.

Habits: male solitary except in rut, female accompanied by young. Feed at night, keeping to thick cover, rest

Footprint of the Wild boar.

by day in lair under fallen tree or rock. Much wallowing in mud and rooting in earth for food. Will turn with ferocity on anyone disturbing it. Hunted extensively and can be dangerous when wounded.

ROE DEER

ORDER	Artiodactyla
FAMILY	Cervidae
GENUS	*Capreolus*
SPECIES	*C. capreolus*

Description: small dainty deer, buck with small, nearly upright antlers, knobbed at base and having

Young Roe deer (1) and the white flash around the tail (2).

only three points and no brow tines, up to 23cm (9in) long, shed in November to December, fully grown and clear of velvet by April or early May. Summer coat bright red-brown, short and smooth. Winter coat becomes long and brittle and changes to warm grey. Underparts, inner sides of thighs and hairs surrounding almost invisible tail, white. Ears relatively large, covered with long hairs and insides whitish. Chin white with white spot on each side of black muzzle. Lips black. Well-grown roe buck about 76cm (2½ft) at shoulder, seldom exceeds 1·2m (4ft) in length, weight up to 32kg (70lb). Doe smaller, up to 21kg (46lb).

Range: across Europe from Mediterranean in south to southern Scandinavia in north and into Asia.

Habitat: prefers open woodlands, sparsely wooded valleys and low mountain slopes, but may be found in almost any area with enough cover.

Life history: mating in late summer, mainly August, but implantation delayed for 3 months. Young, usually twins, born in May and June,

Roe deer *Capreolus capreolus*.

spotted for first year only. After two weeks doe and young rejoin buck, forming family party until end of winter when young usually driven away.

Feeding: predominantly browses, leaves of trees and shrubs but also grass, fungi, berries, acorns and

Male Roe deer with antlers 'in velvet' (1) and third year (2), second year (3), and first year (4) growth stages.

beechmast in winter. Habit of eating tips of young tree shoots and fraying bark with antlers often causes damage to new plantations. Can also cause damage to rose trees and other plants in gardens. Said to eat 3—4 % of its own weight daily.

Habits: feeds mainly at dusk and dawn lying up in cover by day. When undisturbed may feed during day. Not easy to see as it moves stealthily through dense cover. Normal gait an easy canter with head held high. Good swimmer. Hearing good, sight and smell not so acute as in Red deer. Both buck and doe have an alarm bark similar to dog. In breeding season doe utters incessant high-pitched squeaking. Quavering and high-pitched scream indicating terror or anguish. Wolf, lynx and Jackal will prey on adult; young taken by foxes and eagles.

Special features: in rutting season, before mating, buck marks a piece of ground in open around a bush or tree by fraying young trees around and scraping ground, occasionally marking scrapes with scent from glands on forehead. Buck chases doe round and round, their hoofs wearing a ring or figure-of-eight in ground (known as roe rings). Leaping recorded 2m (6ft 6in) vertical, about 7m (21ft) horizontal.

MIXED WOODLANDS

Mixed woodlands constitute an environment that is in many ways intermediate between coniferous forests and broadleaved woodlands. Their northern limit is marked by the pedunculate oak and varies between latitudes 56°N and 61°N, being farthest north in Sweden and Finland and farthest south towards the Urals.

The origin of such mixed forests can only be drawn in broad outline. After the Ice Age the retreating ice cap left behind a sodden earth and extensive marshes, such as are found today in the Pripet Marshes, the Masurian lakes and, more widely distributed, the numerous lakes and marshes in Finland. The subsequent drying out made possible the invasion of vegetation. The pioneers in this would have been the low-growing herbs and woody plants such as heather and bilberry. These need considerable amounts of sunlight and are capable of rapid growth. The fate of the taller shrubs and trees that followed, the successors as they are called, depended on numerous factors and it was the interplay of these that determined whether a particular area would support conifers or broadleaved trees as the climax vegetation.

In general, the invasion of the belt south of the taiga in Europe followed a distinct pattern. The broadleaved trees came in from the west, the conifers from the east — from northern Asia, beyond the Urals. Birch is the foremost broadleaved tree of the mixed forest: others include the oak, maple, lime, alder, mountain ash, aspen and hazel. The progress of the individual species is linked with the types of seeds they produce. The birch, for example, produces prodigious quantities of small seeds which are freely carried everywhere by the wind. Acorns tend to fall and settle in the vicinity of the parent tree and their spread is dependent on being carried by animals. Once the seeds have settled, and this applies equally to the seeds of conifers and broadleaved trees, much depends on the nature of the soil, whether sand, loam, chalky or gravel, and on the pioneers already established. Scots pine seedlings, for example, quickly become established in short heather but cannot compete with tall heather and are at a disadvantage where moss has taken over. Birch seedlings are small and cannot compete with grass. Poplar and willow seedlings, even smaller and more selective, will

colonize only bare ground that is moist when they ripen in summer. The acorn has the very great advantage of carrying a massive food reserve, and it can send a strong tap root down through a mat of grass and push its sturdy shoot up through a cover of herbaceous plants, which doubtless accounts for the oak being predominant at the frontier between the taiga and the mixed woodlands.

Feeding relationships. Much of the invertebrate leaf litter fauna found in broadleaved woodland is not found in mixed woods.

Earthworms, in particular, seem susceptible to the presence of conifers. Insects and arachnids, however, still proliferate and support an abundance of insectivorous birds. Tits are particularly common, searching pine cones for larvae of night-flying moths, but Nuthatches and Tree-creepers are found less frequently. Few insectivorous mammals have succeeded in this environment, the only notable species being the Brown bear. This animal is primarily a vegetarian (feeding on roots) though it often takes large insects and occasionally birds. Several

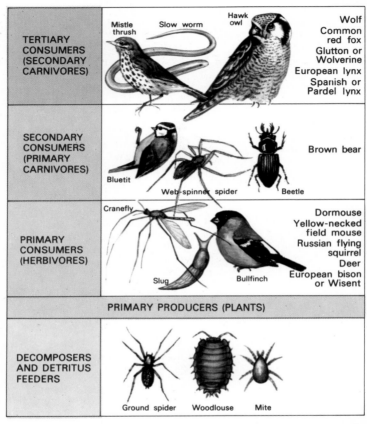

TERTIARY CONSUMERS (SECONDARY CARNIVORES)	Mistle thrush, Slow worm, Hawk owl	Wolf, Common red fox, Glutton or Wolverine, European lynx, Spanish or Pardel lynx
SECONDARY CONSUMERS (PRIMARY CARNIVORES)	Bluetit, Web-spinner spider, Beetle	Brown bear
PRIMARY CONSUMERS (HERBIVORES)	Cranefly, Slug, Bullfinch	Dormouse, Yellow-necked field mouse, Russian flying squirrel, Deer, European bison or Wisent
PRIMARY PRODUCERS (PLANTS)		
DECOMPOSERS AND DETRITUS FEEDERS	Ground spider, Woodlouse, Mite	

mammals are evident among the herbivores, notably the Dormouse, Yellow-neck mouse and Flying squirrel, feeding on beech, hazel and chestnut fruits supplemented with pine cones.

Among the secondary carnivores owls assume a greater importance, foreshadowing their dominance in pure conifer forests, but several large predatory mammals flourish, particularly Wolves and Lynxes where there are deer herds. Red foxes are sometimes insectivorous, taking carabid beetles, but they feed mainly on small rodents and birds.

Flying squirrel *Pteromys volans*.

RUSSIAN FLYING SQUIRREL

ORDER	Rodentia
FAMILY	Sciuridae
GENUS	*Pteromys*
SPECIES	*P. volans*

Description: general form similar to that of Red squirrel, with furred gliding membrane extending from fore- to hindleg on each side. A cartilaginous spur on each wrist pulls membranes taut when gliding. Upperparts grey to brown, underparts white. Snout blunt, whiskers long, eyes large, ears small. Tail flattened, feathered. Head and body length 150–170mm (6–7in), tail 95–130mm (4–5in), weight less than 100g (4oz).

Range: northern Asiatic species extending into northern Russia and Finland.

Habitat: deciduous or coniferous or mixed forests.

Life history: similar to that of Red squirrel with two litters a year of 3–6 young.

Feeding: food includes tree seeds (acorns, chestnuts), buds, berries, fruit, fungi.

Habits: nocturnal, rests by day in hole in a tree. Climbs tree to glide up to 45·7m (50yds) to next tree, using gliding membranes. Hibernates. Voice a screech. Prey of martens and owls.

Garden or Oak dormouse *Eliomys quercinus*.

GARDEN OR OAK DORMOUSE

ORDER	Rodentia
FAMILY	Gliridae
GENUS	*Eliomys*
SPECIES	*E. quercinus*

Description: one of most attractive of dormice characterised by long, slender, black tufted tail and conspicuous black face mask. Large ears. Fur greyish-brown with some white above, underparts white. Head and body length 100–170mm (4–6¾in), tail 80–95mm (3–3¾in), weight 45–120g (1½–4oz).

Range: France to European Russia, south to Mediterranean and North Africa. Especially common in Mediterranean regions.

Habitat: deciduous or coniferous woodlands with scrub layer, orchards and large gardens. Spends more time on ground than other dormice and often found among rocks. Up to 2000m (6500ft).

Life-history: gestation about 23 days, one or two litters a year with usually 3–6 young each. Eyes open 3 weeks, weaned by 4 weeks. Longevity up to 5 years.

Feeding: omnivorous, eating larger proportion of animal food than other dormice, including insects, snails, birds' eggs and young mammals. Also fruits and nuts and sometimes said to store food in autumn. May do considerable damage to fruit crops in orchards.

Habits: nocturnal, sometimes active in the morning. Spends day in nest in hole or under tree roots, in cleft in rock or in wall. Most vocal member of family, uttering clucking and churring noise. Often enters buildings especially in autumn. Hibernates early, often in September, reawakens in April.

FOREST DORMOUSE

ORDER	Rodentia
FAMILY	Gliridae
GENUS	*Dryomys*
SPECIES	*D. nitedula*

Description: greyish or yellowish-brown fur on back, white underneath, with conspicuous black face mask, bushy tail. Head and body length 80–130mm (3–5in), tail 80–95mm (3–3¾in).

Range: 2 separate areas: (1) from Switzerland to Austria almost to the Urals and from southern Poland to whole of Balkans (not in peninsular Italy). (2) Asia Minor and Israel to north-western India and Chinese Turkestan.

Habitat: in Europe deciduous woodland with thick scrub layer (eg hazel) but up to 1500m (5000ft) in Alps.

Life-history: breeding between April and July. Gestation about 24 days. Normally one litter a year with usually 3–6 young.

Feeding: fruits, seeds, insects.

Habits: strictly nocturnal. Compact nests built of twigs in branches up to 6m (20ft) from ground. In Europe, hibernates from October until April in tree holes or underground, occasionally in buildings.

Forest dormouse *Dryomys nitedula*.

YELLOW-NECKED FIELD MOUSE

ORDER	Rodentia
FAMILY	Muridae
GENUS	*Apodemus*
SPECIES	*A. flavicollis*

Description: similar to Wood mouse but slightly larger and more robust and vigorous. Upperparts reddish-brown, whitish below. Brown chest spot between forelegs extends into yellow or orange collar, sometimes extending back along lower flanks. Yellow collar fades away towards southern and eastern Europe. Head and body length up to nearly 124mm (5in) with tail of similar length, weight about 34g (1¼oz).

Range: Europe, North Africa, southwest and central Asia, northern India but absent from large areas.

Habitat: mature woodland. More arboreal than Wood mouse and has been recorded in canopy of forest. Also extends to higher altitudes than Wood mouse. Readily enters houses.

Life history: little known but probably similar to Wood mouse.

Feeding: seeds, grain, acorns, nuts, fruit. Food hoarded.

Habits: nocturnal, more energetic and better jumper than Wood mouse. Raids apple stores and in autumn takes nuts into houses, taking them up cavity walls to store them in upper stories under floorboards. Preyed upon by many mammals and birds.

Special features: sometimes population explosions after mild winter as in Yugoslavia in 1967 when Yellow-necks and Wood mice swarmed out in tens of thousands from woodlands onto arable land, damaging crops and even entering farmhouses and buildings.

Yellow-necked field mouse
Apodemus flavicollis.

WOLF

ORDER	Carnivora
FAMILY	Canidae
GENUS	*Canis*
SPECIES	*C. lupus*

Description: large, dog-like, with dropping, bushy tail, broad chest, small pointed ears and long legs. Typical colour yellowish- or brownish-grey brindled with black. Black or white individuals occasionally recorded. Size and colour vary with locality. Head and body length up to 140cm (4½ft), tail up to 41cm (16in), height at shoulder up to 80cm (31½in), weight up to 50kg (110lb). Bitch smaller.

Range: much reduced in numbers. Wiped out in most of Europe except wilder parts of Scandinavia, Iberia, central France, Italy and Balkans; Asia, North America.

Habitat: forests, mountains and tundra.

Life history: breeding season January to March, gestation 60–63 days. Usually 5–6 blind cubs in litter in burrow, cave or enlarged fox earth. Eyes open 9 days, weaned 8 weeks. Both parents help in rearing and feeding. Stay together as family party.

Feeding: typically feed on larger ungulates, eg Reindeer, Elk, deer and also domestic animals as well as smaller mammals.

Habits: solitary, in pairs or small

family parties, hunting over fixed territory by day, often travelling extensively, denning up by night in rocky chamber, under roots of tree, or in holes dug in ground. In summer family party remains together, in winter several parties may combine for hunting. Well-known howl used to call members of party or troop together. Also barks, growls and yelps. Stories of large packs probably refer to troops made up of family parties brought together by hunger.

Wolf *Canis lupus*.

Food of the Wolf: (1) small mammals, (2) birds, (3) occasionally tubers and roots and (4) large mammals.

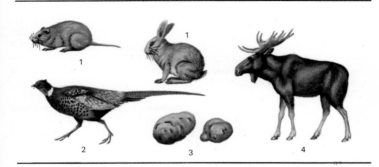

RED FOX

ORDER	Carnivora
FAMILY	Canidae
GENUS	*Vulpes*
SPECIES	*V. vulpes*

Description: muzzle sharp, pointed, ears erect (pricked), eye with elliptical, vertical pupil; 5 toes on forefeet, 4 on hindfeet. Claws not retractile. Dog-fox and vixen similar but vixen smaller, lacks cheek ruffs, shorter coat; fur sandy to brownish red, greyish-white underparts, black on fronts of limbs and backs of ear, tail bushy, forming a brush, with white (rarely black) tip or tag; colour may change with annual moult (July to August) when adults become thin-bodied, long-legged with slender tail, then hard to distinguish from growing cubs. Underfur re-grown last so coat thickens as winter approaches. Average head and body length of dog-fox just over 60cm (24in), tail 40cm (16in). Height at

Food of the Red fox: (1) mice, (2) rabbits, (3) fruit, (4) birds, (5) beetles, (6) large mammals and (7) invertebrates.

shoulder 35cm (14in). Average dog-fox weighs 6·8kg (15lb), vixen 5·4kg (12lb). Records greatly in excess of these measurements especially in Scotland.

Range: Europe, northwest Africa, Asia south to central India, sea-level to 4267m (14,000ft).

Habitat: typically woodlands but highly variable, lowlands to mountains, scrub, farmland, sea cliffs, disused mines, towns, even large cities, railway marshalling yards.

Life history: mating, late December to February, preceded by pre-nuptial play. Gestation 51–52 days. Single litter a year born in 'earth', usually March–April but any time from November to July, with usually 4 cubs weighing 100g (3½oz), with chocolate-brown woolly fur for first month. Adult

Red fox *Vulpes vulpes*.

pelage by autumn. Eyes open at 10 days. First appear above ground at $3\frac{1}{2}$ weeks, weaned at 8–10 weeks but start taking solid food before this. Dog-fox brings food from moment of birth and continues this after weaning. Play between cubs similar to adults' pre-nuptial play. Dog-fox plays much with cubs. Vixen and occasionally dog-fox take cubs hunting. Cubs leave parents 7–8 weeks. Reach adult size at 6 months, sexually mature by December.

Feeding: prey taken by stalking, with final pounce; mice (swallowed whole) seized by fox rising on hindlegs and dropping forepaws first on prey. Surplus food cached in hole scraped with forepaw, covered with earth pushed with nose-tip. Food: rats, mice, voles, Rabbits, Hedgehogs, squirrels, frogs, snails, beetles, grasshoppers, small birds, eggs (game-birds, poultry and lambs killed locally where parents feed cubs on these), grass, fruits (especially blackberry and bilberry), carrion, will dig out offal buried 0·5m (2ft) deep; eggs up to goose size buried singly for later use.

Habits: solitary except in breeding season. Most of day passed in 'earth', cavity in ground either made by fox, or Badger set or Rabbit's burrow taken over. Nest sometimes in tree, eg on crown of pollarded tree, up to 4·3m (14ft) from ground. Hunts usually at night but can be seen in daytime. Swims well and sometimes climbs trees. Foxes use a great variety of calls: most familiar is high sharp bark of both dog-fox and vixen, especially in winter; wailing scream by vixen, also occasionally by dog; chiddering when playing or in courtship.

Special features: Senses: smell, hearing, sight (even in daytime) acute. Despite hunting, shooting, trapping and poisoning by man, numbers not significantly diminished. Now fox is known to carry rabies future prospects are uncertain.

BROWN BEAR

ORDER	Carnivora
FAMILY	Ursidae
GENUS	*Ursus*
SPECIES	*U. arctos*

Description: heavy build, practically tailless, broad flat feet with 5 toes and non-retractile claws; well-developed snout, wet nose, prominent forehead, small but conspicuous ears, cheek teeth weak, flattened. Coat shaggy, brown, varying in shade from very dark brown to pale creamy fawn. Average head and body length 1·82m (6ft), maximum 2·13m (7ft), weight 90–250kg (200–550lb). Heavier in eastern Europe.

Range: in Europe small numbers in wilder parts of Pyrenees, Carpathians, Italian Alps, Balkans, Scandinavia; more plentiful in USSR, Asia, North America.

Habitat: wild and mountainous country, coniferous and deciduous forests.

Life history: rut in July, male then leaves female, gestation 180–250 days, normally two cubs born every second year, in winter den in January or February during hibernation, very small, helpless, hairless and blind at birth 203mm (8in) long, weight 350g (12½oz). Leave den with mother in spring, weaned 4 months. Sexual maturity 2 years. Longevity 34 years.

Feeding: omnivorous; food largely vegetable: roots, tubers, bulbs, berries, nuts, fungi, grain. Animal food includes small mammals, birds' eggs, fish, very occasionally larger mammals such as deer and domestic stock. Particularly fond of wild honey, grubs and combs also eaten.

Brown bear *Ursus arctos.*

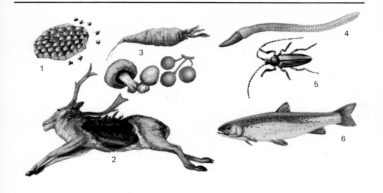

Food of the Brown bear: (1) honey, (2) occasionally large mammals, (3) fruit and vegetables, (4) invertebrates, (5) beetles and (6) fish.

During autumn feeds voraciously on fruit and berries, accumulating fat in preparation for hibernation.

Habits: solitary, active mainly at night especially in inhabited country. Sight poor, senses of smell and hearing acute. Ambling gait, runs and trots over long distances, climbs occasionally, slowly and deliberately, swims well. Grunts and howls when angry. Hibernates during winter in holes in rocks, caves or under tree roots, male and female separately. Female usually one year with young, second year alone during which more cubs born. Hiber-

nation, or winter dormancy, fairly complete but little reduction in temperature and sleep light, no food taken.

Special features: matter of opinion whether there are many species of Brown bears distributed over Europe, Asia and North America or whether there is only one. View nowadays is that Brown bears of North America and Asia all belong to same species *Ursus arctos*.

Brown bears have been so heavily persecuted in Europe that their size is now much smaller than formerly. In extreme eastern Europe where they are still fairly numerous they are much heavier, reflected in weight of cubs which in western Europe is only about 350g (12½oz) but elsewhere may go up to 680g (1½lb).

GLUTTON OR WOLVERINE

ORDER	Carnivora
FAMILY	Mustelidae
GENUS	*Gulo*
SPECIES	*G. gulo*

Description: largest of mustelids, looking like something between

marten and bear. Shaggy coat of thick dense fur, very dark brown above with pale brown band on sides and dark brown below. Powerfully built, thick bodied, short legs set wide apart ending in broad powerful paws armed with long sharp claws. Very powerful teeth and jaws. Full grown male up to 1·2m (4ft) including 0·3m (1ft) of tail. Height at shoulder 355–430mm (14–17in). Weight 13·6–27·2kg (30–60lb).

Range: across arctic and subarctic Europe and Asia and in North America from Arctic to northern United States.

Habitat: cold evergreen forests 250–4000m (800–13,000ft) above sea level. In summer northernmost animals leave forests and scrub and wander on tundra.

Life history: mate in autumn. Probably delayed implantation as young not born until Feruary to March or even May. Usually 2 or 3, occasionally 5, young born with thick woolly fur. Weaned 8–10 weeks. Stay with mother for as long as 2 years, then she drives them away to find own territories. Sexually mature at 4 years. Has lived in captivity for 16 years.

Feeding: hunts alone or in pairs, mainly at night. Little skill in stalking. Drives other predators from their food. Carrion-eaters, they have strong teeth and jaws, can crack large bones to powder. Sometimes robs traps. Said to eat more than needs but has large stomach. Uneaten food cached. Food includes carrion, mice, rats, small mammals of any kind, eggs, ground-nesting birds, ducks, snails, fruit, berries. Said to be powerful enough to kill Reindeer or Elk.

Habits: mainly nocturnal or possibly may have 3–4 hourly rhythm of activity and rest. Does not make permanent home or burrow but uses

Glutton or Wolverine *Gulo gulo*.

Food of the Wolverine: (1) small mammals, (2) occasionally larger mammals, (3) rabbits and hares, (4) vegetables, (5) birds and (6) fruits.

whatever shelter is available including man-made. Young born in hollow tree, among rocks or even in snow drift. Capable of climbing trees but stays mostly on ground. Cannot move with speed. Ferocious and courageous in driving other predators from food, even bears. Growls and hisses when angry, grunts and squeals when playing. Few natural enemies. Persecuted by man for its destructiveness and for reputation for killing Reindeer. Eskimos hunt it for its fur.

Populations: although numbers reduced everywhere by persecution still not uncommon in parts of its range.

LYNX OR NORTHERN LYNX

ORDER	Carnivora
FAMILY	Felidae
GENUS	*Lynx*
SPECIES	*L. lynx*

Description: medium-sized, long-legged member of Felidae (some authors prefer to call it *Felis lynx*) with conspicuous ear-tufts and face-ruffs. Coat rufous with variable number of dark spots, mainly on limbs, spots often indistinct. Tail short, outer third black. Head and body length 80–130cm (32–52in), tail 11–24·5cm (4–10in), height at shoulder 60–75cm (24–30in), weight 18–38kg (40–84lb).

Range: formerly from taiga (northern Europe) to Mediterranean, now exterminated except in Scandinavia. Also found in Asia and North America.

139

Lynx or Northern lynx *Lynx lynx.*

Habitat: woods on rocky ground, now mainly in mountains.

Life history; mate in early spring. Gestation 60–76 days. Single litter a year of 1–4 (usually 2–3) kittens, born in March–April which stay with mother through first winter, reach sexual maturity at two years. Eyes open 10–12 days.

Feeding: main prey is hares, Rabbits and ground birds, young deer (also young of domestic stock), often from ambush. Usual tactics are stalking followed by a final dash, using a throat bite with larger prey. Carrion also eaten and cannibalism has been reported. In Sweden Reindeer taken in winter, elsewhere Roe deer.

Food of the Lynx: (1) small mammals, (2) hedgehogs, (3) deer, (4) fish and (5) birds.

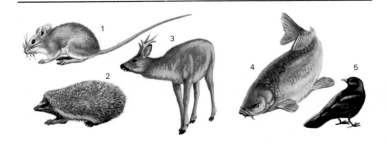

Pardel or Spanish lynx *Lynx pardina*.

Habits: solitary, a single male may have territory of 300sq km (115sq mi) but a female may occupy a smaller territory within this. Nocturnal, becoming active after sunset, terrestrial but can climb, although not to any great height. Dens up by day in a dense thicket, a hollow tree or under an overhanging rock. Voice mainly a hiss or a scold. Mating call of male a howl ending in a moan.

PARDEL OR SPANISH LYNX

ORDER	Carnivora
FAMILY	Felidae
GENUS	*Lynx*
SPECIES	*L. pardina*

Description: similar to Northern lynx and regarded by some authorities as belonging to same species. Differences between two are that Pardel lynx is slightly smaller and more heavily spotted. Typical locality is Spain, including Coto Doñana and Pyrenees but heavily spotted lynx also occur in Carpathians, Balkans and Caucasus. Size and shape of spots and distribution on body variable from one individual to another so that there appear to be intermediates between Northern and Pardel lynx. Argument for keeping the two species separate is that they are genetically distinct. Thus, according to B. Kurten, Spanish lynx in Pleistocene ranged farther north and its distribution overlapped that of Northern lynx and that interbreeding did not occur.

North American lynx is now regarded as conspecific with *Lynx lynx* which gives that species a range that formerly covered Europe, much of Asia and northern North America. This suggests that Spanish lynx can be little more than a subspecies, or even a local race.

Fallow deer *Dama dama*.

FALLOW DEER

ORDER	Artiodactyla
FAMILY	Cervidae
GENUS	*Dama*
SPECIES	*D. dama*

Description: distinguished by palmate antlers, flattened and expanded in all branches of upper part but main stem or 'beam' rounded. Antlers worn only by buck. Fully developed by sixth year. Shed annually in May, new antlers fully grown and clear of velvet by end of August. Many colour varieties. Most usual summer coat deep fawn or reddish-yellow above, spotted with white and with yellowish-white underparts. Vertical white stripe on either side of rump shows up when animal in retreat. Winter coat greyish-brown, change takes place in October. Black tail

142

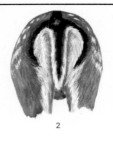

with white underside kept in constant motion from side to side. Black variety with spots almost obscured fairly common. No upper canine teeth and first upper incisor expanded. Average height of buck at shoulder 91cm (3ft). Hind slightly smaller. Length of antler 65–78cm (25–31in).

Range: western Europe up to 60°N latitude. Asia Minor. Distribution influenced by introductions by man; original range difficult to ascertain.

Habitat: deciduous or mixed woodlands with scrub layer and grassy glades. Kept extensively in deer parks from which escapes made.

Life history: rut starts in October when bucks gather does into harems. Noisy challenging. Rhythmic grunting noise rather than roar.

Footprints of Fallow deer.

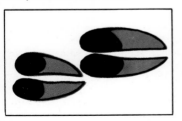

Winter colouration of Fallow deer (1) and detail of flash (2).

Old bucks mark rutting area to be defended by fraying young trees with antlers and urinating in scrapes beneath them. Younger males establish territories downwind of these. Rut lasts about a month, does 2 years or older become pregnant. Gestation 8 months. One fawn, occasionally 2, rarely 3, able to run within a few hours of birth if necessary. After rut mixed herds remain together until spring when males leave.

Feeding: mainly grasses and herbs, nuts, berries. In winter browses young shoots and kills many small trees by eating bark. Sometimes causes damage to cultivated crops of turnips, beet etc.

Habits: feeds mainly at dawn and dusk but can be seen in daytime especially in winter. Old bucks mainly nocturnal and rarely seen. Mixed herds in winter led by doe, and it is does that protect herd. Safety sought in cover rather than flight. Gait stilted and jerky but herds move usually in single file at a steady shuffling gallop. Usually silent except for males grunting call in rut and bark of alarm. Bleat of fawns. Foxes main predators of young fawns.

143

Red deer *Cervus elaphus*.

RED DEER

ORDER	Artiodactyla
FAMILY	Cervidae
GENUS	*Cervus*
SPECIES	*C. elaphus*

Description: summer coat reddish-brown. Changes to brownish-grey in winter by new growth of grey hairs, rougher and thicker. Considerable variations in colour. Underparts white with patch of white round tail as 'recognition mark'. Tail tufted, often with black central streak. Stag develops mane of long brown hair during rut. Calves variable, usually brown flecked with white. Males only bear antlers, start-ing as simple spikes or knobs in first year, additional points appearing on main body of antler until there may be more than 12. Occasional males, known as hummels, with no points above brow tine or no antlers at all. Preorbital glands used by both sexes for marking territory. Antlers cast February to April (younger in-dividuals later). Coat moulted in May. New antlers grown and clean of velvet by end of August. Fully-grown stag, up to 1·4m (4½ft) at shoulder. Weight varies with habitat. European forests: up to 254kg (560lb), English woodlands: up to 190kg (420lb), Scottish moors: up to 95kg (210lb). Antlers also variable, average 100cm (39½in) long; 75cm (30in) span; 125mm (5in) beam; 7kg (15lb) in weight per pair.

Range: discontinuous across Europe and Asia, in Europe from Arctic Circle southwards; also North Africa (Barbary stag).

Habitat: true home, dense deciduous forest, especially forest margin. Sometimes forced to live in open woodlands and on moors.

Life history: rut, September to October. Stags round up hinds and guard harems from other stags, roaring frequently. Wallow in peat bogs and muddy pools before and during rut. Gestation 8 months. Peak of calving end of May and June. Normally only one calf, occasionally twins, already covered with hair. Can run within a few hours. Weaning begins at one month but suckling continues for 8 to 10 months. Male calves remain with hind until second

Winter colouration of Red deer (1) and growth stages (2) of the antlers found only in the male.

Young Red deer (1) and detail of flash (2).

autumn, females permanently with mother's herd and reach sexual maturity in third year; males normally do not breed until fourth year. Longevity 20 years.

Feeding: browsers rather than grazers. Feeding mainly at dawn and dusk on leaves and young shoots of deciduous trees and shrubs. Nuts, acorns, lichens, berries, fungi also eaten. In open country, grass, heather, bilberry; fruits in autumn. Seaweed on coasts. On farmland, root crops and vegetables. During rut stags eat little.

Habits: day spent resting on hill or in shade of woodland, greatest ac-

tivity dusk and early morning. Where little disturbed, not markedly nocturnal. Young calves taken by foxes, Golden eagles and Wild cats. Adult deer taken by Wolves. Main enemy man, because prized as a game animal. Roaring mostly confined to stags during rut. Stags will bark when frightened. Hinds bark warning, nasal bleat when alarmed. Calf, when alarmed, gives high-pitched bleat or scream.

Special features: predominantly social species but size of herds varies greatly. Outside rutting season, females and immature males form herds, about 20, in woodland, possibly over 100 in open country. Distinct social hierarchy in herd. Mature

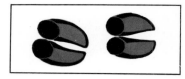

Footprints of Red deer.

stags form independent herds, much less stable than those of hinds. Often males solitary in woodland. Function of antlers still problematic, possibly indication of rank rather than means of defence. May be used in fights between rival stags but main force of encounter is in butting with forehead. Usual gait a steady trot or lazy stride, gallop used only in moments of alarm or imminent danger.

EUROPEAN BISON OR WISENT

ORDER	Artiodactyla
FAMILY	Bovidae
GENUS	*Bison*
SPECIES	*B. bonasus*

Description: large ruminant with shaggy coat of long brown hair; horns worn by both bulls and cows. By comparison with better known North American buffalo (*B. bison*), coat is shorter and shoulder hump

Food of the Bison: (1) grasses and low herbs, (2) shoots, (3) bark and (4) fungi.

less pronounced. Head and body length of bull nearly 2·7m (9ft), tail 80cm (32in), height at shoulder 1·8m (5ft), weight 850kg (1900lb); cows smaller.

Range: up to 16th century extended throughout deciduous forests zone including southern Sweden but not British Isles. Now extinct in

1   2   3   4

Bison or Wisent *Bison bonasus*.

wild but a small herd remains in Bialowieza Forest, in Poland, enclosed and protected.

Life history: gestation 276 days. Single young born May to June, weaned September, reaches sexual maturity at 2½ years, fully grown at 6 years.

Feeding: browses leaves of oak, elm, willow, chiefly.; takes acorns in autumn, browses heathers and evergreen shrubs in winter, takes grass rarely.

Habits: cows and calves form herds of 20–30, bulls solitary, join herds at rut.

Special features: species extinct as wild animal by 1925. Present herd of 300–400 built up from individuals in parks and zoos.

CONIFEROUS FORESTS

Coniferous forests occur north of the broadleaved woodlands where winters are long and cold. They lie mainly between 45°N and 70°N and extend over 1500 million hectares (3700 million acres). The most dominant trees are conifers such as spruces, firs, pines and larch which have needle leaves that are more resistant to winter cold and drought than are those of broadleaved trees.

Virgin coniferous forests occur in Scandinavia and Finland where, towards the end of the Ice Age, the land was largely covered by sea. They grow on ground composed of peat bogs and of gravels, boulders and sand deposited by the melting glaciers. Farther south man has destroyed large areas of deciduous trees, and even where areas of forest have persisted he has replaced the original broadleaved trees with the quickgrowing conifers to achieve a more rapid return from his forestry.

Unlike broadleaved trees, conifers can grow as soon as winter is over and so are better adapted to exploit regions where the vegetative season is short. To maintain growth, deciduous trees need about 120 days per year with a mean temperature over 10°C (50°F), while conifers

can manage with 30 days, although there are differences between species. The narrow, conical, monopodial tree form with drooping branches is adaptive to regions of high snowfall.

Apart from a scattering of bright flowers during the spring, there is little seasonal change in coniferous forests. Except for the larch, which sheds all its leaves in autumn, conifers shed their leaves in relatively small quantities at all times of the year but more abundantly in early summer. There is, therefore, a more or less continuous 'rain' of needles which effectively smothers the surface of the earth below, forming a most effective mulch inhibiting the growth of most vegetation. In addition, the decomposition of the needles imparts an acidity to the soil so that, once introduced, conifers suppress seedling oak, beech and other broadleaved trees, as well as the majority of herbaceous plants.

Conifers are fast-growing relative to the broadleaved trees. They seldom, if ever, show hollow cavities in the trunk or branches. Their bark is so structured that there is nothing to compare with the loose bark found on many broadleaved trees which is

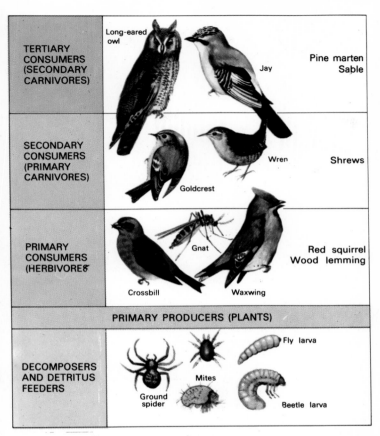

TERTIARY CONSUMERS (SECONDARY CARNIVORES)	Long-eared owl	Jay	Pine marten Sable
SECONDARY CONSUMERS (PRIMARY CARNIVORES)	Goldcrest	Wren	Shrews
PRIMARY CONSUMERS (HERBIVORES)	Crossbill	Gnat Waxwing	Red squirrel Wood lemming
PRIMARY PRODUCERS (PLANTS)			
DECOMPOSERS AND DETRITUS FEEDERS	Ground spider	Mites	Fly larva Beetle larva

so important a factor in the ecology of bats, which often roost under it. Moreover the absence of an undergrowth means a lack of diversified fruits and little in the way of fodder. Insects, also, are relatively few in both population numbers and numbers of species, an important factor for small mammals such as shrews.

Feeding relationships. As we have seen, in coniferous forests, the leaf litter associated with deciduous forests is replaced by a dense blanket of coniferous needles. This blanket does not encourage insect life which is therefore limited except for swarms of gnats and mosquitoes (the larvae of which are aquatic) and some carabid ground beetles. It is not surprising, therefore, that there are few insectivores. Among the passerines only tits, wrens and goldcrests occur to any great extent with little competition from the sporadic shrew species. Where animal food is scarce, shrews often turn to vegetable sources, particularly fir and pine

149

seeds. They will also take carrion if it is reasonably fresh.

Herbivores are more diverse, with several seed-eating bird species, notably the crossbills and grosbeaks. Among mammals the Red squirrel takes mainly seeds of Scots pine though also buds, berries, bulbs and

roots of many other species. It will also occasionally take eggs and young of small birds. The paucity of animals is continued among the secondary carnivores where only some marten species succeed against the ruthless efficiency of the larger owls and hawks.

MASKED OR LAXMANN'S SHREW

ORDER	Insectivora
FAMILY	Soricidae
GENUS	*Sorex*
SPECIES	*S. caecutiens*

Masked shrew *Sorex caecutiens*.

Description: vernacular name doubtful; called Masked shrew by van den Brink on supposed affinity with North American species of that name. Similar to Common shrew in form, habits and life history. Differs in lacking light brown flanks and in size. Upperparts brown, underparts white, with white extending well up on flanks. Head and body length 44–67mm ($1\frac{3}{4}$–$2\frac{4}{5}$in), tail 31–44mm ($1\frac{1}{4}$–$1\frac{4}{5}$in), weight 3·5–7g ($\frac{1}{8}$–$\frac{1}{4}$oz).

Range: Asiatic species that extends into northern Russia, Finland, northern Sweden; also into Poland.

Habitat: coniferous woods; also on tundra.

LEAST SHREW

ORDER	Insectivora
FAMILY	Soricidae
GENUS	*Sorex*
SPECIES	*S. minutissimus*

Description: similar to Pygmy shrew but with relatively short tail. Head and body length 35–53mm ($1\frac{2}{5}$–2in), tail 21–32mm($\frac{7}{8}$–$1\frac{1}{4}$in), weight 1·5–4g ($\frac{1}{7}$oz) or less. Little is known of their habits and ecology: in Europe only solitary specimens have been found in Finland, Karelia, Valdai Hills and Moscow Province.

RED SQUIRREL

ORDER	Rodentia
FAMILY	Sciuridae
GENUS	*Sciurus*
SPECIES	*S. vulgaris*

Description: summer coat rufous with dark mid-dorsal stripe, winter coat brownish-grey, underparts white. Fur softer and thicker in winter and ear tufts longer and bushy. Hairs of tail and ear-tufts shed once a year. Tail may have cream tint in summer. Tail more feathered than bushy, hairs extending outwards and backwards on each side. Muzzle

Red squirrel *Sciurus vulgaris.*

well equipped with whiskers. Prominent eyes black and bright. Large pointed tufted ears. Hindlegs much longer than forelimbs. Feet well adapted for climbing. Forefeet have four toes and rudimentary 'thumb' and hindfeet have five toes. Soles hairy and long curved claws are needle-sharp. Sexes alike. Young moult into appropriate seasonal coat after weaning. Juvenile colouring as in adult. Albinos rare. Adults, average head and body length 219mm (8·7in), tail 182mm (7·2in), weight 260–345g (9–12oz).

Range: throughout most wooded parts of Europe south to Mediterranean, from Ireland in west to Japan in east. In north it extends beyond Arctic Circle into birch scrub dividing taiga and tundra. Throughout this area number of subspecies recognised.

Habitat: typically in coniferous woodlands but also in mixed woods. Favours shelter and seclusion.

Life history: breeding period depends on quantity of food available and on weather conditions. Two main seasons in south, January to April and late May to August. Gestation about 46 days. Mating associated with much chasing and a chattering call. 1–6 (usually 3–4) young in litter, born blind and naked weighing 12g (less than 5oz). Develop hair at one week, lower incisors erupt third week, first set of teeth complete about 10 weeks. Fourth and fifth weeks, eyes and ears open. Weaned at 7 to 10 weeks. First moult at 15 weeks, second moult at 7 months. Young remain with parents until adult. Sexual maturity between 6 and 11 months.

Feeding: mainly vegetarian. Food stored by burying singly or in groups. Re-location by smell. Damage done to young pines by taking bark from leader shoots. Food: seeds of trees especially of conifers, others including acorns, beechmast, chestnuts and hazel nuts, buds in spring, fungi, wild cherries, wild strawberries, bilberries, insects and birds' eggs, nestlings more rarely.

Habits: nests (dreys) in branches of trees, bulky structures of twigs, strips of bark, moss and leaves; cup-shaped or domed. May use several nests for sleeping at night. Sometimes converts disused nests of crows or magpies. Breeding nest a huge ball of sticks and leaves, sometimes in roomy hollow in tree trunk. Diurnal with activity peaks in early

Nest of the Red squirrel.

morning and before dusk, minor peak at midday. Cold weather inhibits activity but no true hibernation. Great agility and speed when climbing and jumping in trees. More hesitant on ground.

Rasping chatter followed by hoarse call or whine. Young have a shrill piping call.

Pine marten and Beech marten principal predators. Eagle owl, where it occurs, principal avian pre-

Food of the Red squirrel: ripe (1) and immature (2) pine seeds, ripe fir seeds (3), ripe (4) and immature (5) Alpine fir cones and hazel nuts (6).

dator. Trapped and exported in large numbers for its fur, especially in eastern Europe. Stoat, Buzzard, Golden eagle and Wild cat may kill some.

Populations: fluctuations in numbers said to follow 7-year cycle; alternatively may follow pine seed fluctuations.

Special features: expert swimmer but only takes to water in exceptional circumstances. Belief that it spreads its tail to act as sail; probably merely holds tail up to keep it dry.

WOOD LEMMING

ORDER	Rodentia
FAMILY	Cricetidae
GENUS	*Myopus*
SPECIES	*M. schisticolor*

Description: short-tailed vole, uniform grey with reddish tinge on back. Head and body length 85–95mm (3½–4in), 15–19mm (⅔in) long, weight about 20–32g (1oz).

Range: central Sweden and Finland.

Habitat: coniferous forests (especially of spruce) with a ground cover of moss.

Life-history: breeds June–August when two litters produced, each of 3–7 young.

Feeding: almost exclusively on mosses, also liverworts, lichens.

Habits: burrows in moss. Fluctuations in numbers, as in Norway lemming, but no marked migrations when numbers high.

Wood lemming *Myopus schisticolor*.

PINE MARTEN

ORDER	Carnivora
FAMILY	Mustelidae
GENUS	*Martes*
SPECIES	*M. martes*

Description: colour varies from rich warm brown to almost black on upper and undersides. Creamy white throat patch, often tinged with orange, sometimes extending up sides of neck. Lithe long body, short legs, sharp claws, broad triangular head with pointed muzzle and pro-

Pine marten *Martes martes*.

minent ears with pale edges, and large, black, prominent eyes. Scent glands near base of tail. Moults from late spring to June with winter moult starting September or October. Very variable in size. Entire length 630–760mm (25–30in) of which 250–280mm (9–12in) is tail, height at shoulder 150mm (6in). Females slightly smaller. Weight: 0·9–1·5kg (2–3½lb).

Range: all wooded regions of Europe and in parts of Asia, north- wards from Mediterranean to limits of tree-growth.

Habitat: mainly arboreal, especially northern conifer belt.

Life history: mating in July and August but implantation delayed until January. Gestation total period c. 270 days. Only one litter per year late March to April with 2–7 young

Food of the Pine marten: (1) squirrels, (2) Rabbits, (3) small mammals, (4) eggs, (5) beetles and other invertebrates, (6) birds and (7) fruit.

(4—5 average), born with thin covering of white or yellowish hair. At 8 days distinct grey stripes appear; these disappear at 20 days. Come out of nest at 2 months old. Weaned 6—7 weeks and soon after leave mother. Mature at 1 year old, produce first litter 2 years old and live up to 17 years (in captivity).

Feeding: hunts singly, in pairs or even groups. Will pursue squirrels and birds in trees but also feeds on ground. Typical carnivore but will also eat fruit and honey. Food includes squirrels, small birds and eggs, occasionally game birds and poultry, Rabbits, voles, hares, rats, mice, caterpillars, beetles, slugs, bees, blackberries, bilberries, cherries. Bees' nests dug up for grubs and honey.

Habits: mainly nocturnal. Dens temporary or permanent, usually in crevices in rocks, old birds' nests, hollow trees. Breeding nest made of grass among rocks, in hollow tree or nest of crow or squirrel or in river bank. Very good climber. Leaps wide distances to land with precision on small foothold. Bounding locomotion on ground. Ferocious and courageous, will attack opponents larger than itself. Secretions from scent glands mark home range. Odour musky, not objectionable, hence alternative name of sweetmart.

Usually silent but uses high-pitched chattering in aggression and a deep huff as alarm note. Mating accompanied by purring and growling. Call of lost cub like tearing of cloth or call of snipe.

Intensively trapped for fur by man. In Britain trapped to preserve game. Occasionally foxes kill them.

Populations: trapped in such large numbers for fur that they have become rare everywhere.

SABLE

ORDER	Carnivora
FAMILY	Mustelidae
GENUS	*Martes*
SPECIES	*M. zibellina*

Description: longish body, moderately short legs, pointed snout, small ears, semi-bushy tail. Fur dark brown, white ill-defined throat patch. Head and body 32—46cm (12—18in), tail 14—18cm (6—7in), weight 0·9—1·8kg (2—4½lb).

Range: mainly northern Asia, extending into N. Russia, N. Finland, N. Sweden.

Habitat: mainly coniferous, sometimes mixed, woods.

Life-history: much play, often apparent fighting, precedes mating July—August. Implantation delayed 7½ months, gestation 1 month, single litter of 1—5, usually 3.

Feeding: mainly small rodents, also ground-living birds, with berries (bilberry, rowanberry) in autumn and seeds of stone pine.

Habits: most are mainly nocturnal, a few individuals mainly diurnal. Solitary, fairly silent, climbs mostly

Sable *Martes zibellina*.

among secondary growth. Extremely agile, leaping from branch to branch, seldom swims. Dens among rocks.

Populations: much reduced through trapping for fur.

MOUNTAINS

Where mountains occur one does not find one particular habitat, but a series of habitats. As one passes from the base to the summit of a mountain, colder weather conditions due to increasing exposure to the elements produce a series of habitats that correspond to environments encountered as one travels towards the North Pole.

The lower slopes or foothills are grass-covered or clothed in broadleaved forest and this gives way to mixed woods and then coniferous forests. After that comes the zone of tundra, which is treeless or with dwarf stunted trees only. The ground is carpeted with low plants having a brief flowering season, with mosses and lichens abundantly intermingled. Finally, there is the snow cap – in those mountains with sufficient altitude – corresponding to polar wastes. The climatic zones of mountains so represented correspond strikingly to the major biotic zones of the lowlands. Where the mountains are high enough to maintain a permanent snow cap, the zone seasonally free of snow, between the summer snowline and the tree line, becomes closely representative of the tundra. The exact height at which one passes from one habitat to another varies with latitude. On Mont Blanc the snowline occurs at 3,000m (9,800ft) and broadleaved forest gives way to coniferous forest at 1,500m (4,900ft).

A second feature of mountains is that, although they form chains, for example across the Pyrenees and Alps, they in fact simulate islands separated by low-lying land. Some animals and plants are restricted to one or another mountain peak or range because distribution from their isolated positions is a chancy and sometimes impossible event.

Feeding relationships. Mountain regions are truly vertebrate dominated. The thin top-soil facilitates the growth of some plants, but low temperatures and the rarified atmosphere slows decomposition processes. Thus insufficient nutrients become available to support a rich invertebrate fauna.

Among the herbivores, mammals are supreme, particularly the Ibex, Mouflon and Chamois. Ibex and Chamois live in large flocks and are extremely efficient in scaling peaks to seek vegetation. The Mouflon tends to exist in smaller groups or as

solitary invividuals and, when young, this may make them vulner- able to predation by marauding eagles.

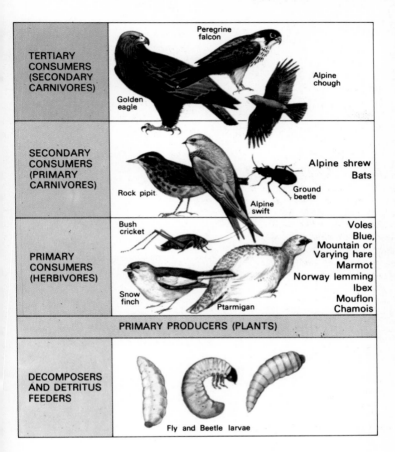

TERTIARY CONSUMERS (SECONDARY CARNIVORES)	Peregrine falcon Golden eagle Alpine chough
SECONDARY CONSUMERS (PRIMARY CARNIVORES)	Rock pipit Alpine swift Ground beetle Alpine shrew Bats
PRIMARY CONSUMERS (HERBIVORES)	Bush cricket Snow finch Ptarmigan Voles Blue, Mountain or Varying hare Marmot Norway lemming Ibex Mouflon Chamois
PRIMARY PRODUCERS (PLANTS)	
DECOMPOSERS AND DETRITUS FEEDERS	Fly and Beetle larvae

However, by far the most important constituent of the eagles' diet is the Mountain hare which also falls prey to buzzards. Marmots are taken by eagles but voles and lemmings tend to be the target of falcons.

There are no secondary carnivorous mammals, the large hawks with their acute vision being far more efficient at spotting and taking prey on precipitous ground. Ravens will also take small mammals and birds. Many small bird species are migrant visitors, so competition from them is sporadic as is their availability as food.

ALPINE SHREW

ORDER	Insectivora
FAMILY	Soricidae
GENUS	*Sorex*
SPECIES	*S. alpinus*

Description: differs from all other European shrews in having a tail about as long as head and body combined, in having five pads on each forefoot instead of six and in having fully developed lateral scent glands in adults of both sexes, each gland with fringes of specialized hairs. Pelage slate-coloured on upperparts, grey-brown underparts. Tail clothed in short hair, dark above, light below. Head and body length 62–77mm ($2\frac{1}{2}$–$3\frac{1}{2}$in), tail 62–75mm ($2\frac{1}{2}$–$3\frac{1}{2}$in), weight 6–10g ($\frac{1}{4}$–$\frac{1}{3}$oz).

Alpine shrew *Sorex alpinus*.

Range: Pyrenees, Alps to Balkan mountains, Bavarian Alps, Sudeten, Tatra and Harz mountains, 600–1500m (1800–4500ft), but near Dresden as low as 180m (540ft).

Habitat: coniferous forests on mountains.

Habits: little known of life history, habits or ecology.

SAVI'S PIPISTRELLE

ORDER	Chiroptera
FAMILY	Vespertilionidae
GENUS	*Pipistrellus*
SPECIES	*P. savii*

Description: very like Common pipistrelle (p. 92) but fur dark with light tips to hairs. Mediterranean region.

NORTHERN BAT

ORDER	Chiroptera
FAMILY	Vespertilionidae
GENUS	*Vespertilio*
SPECIES	*V. nilssoni*

Description: head and body 48–54mm (2in), tail 38–47mm ($1\frac{1}{2}$in), forearm 37–42mm ($1\frac{1}{2}$in), weight 8–13g ($\frac{1}{4}$oz). Otherwise very like Serotine except for golden gloss on upperparts and yellowish underparts. Scandinavia, eastern Europe, small areas in central Europe.

Savi's pipistrelle *Pipistrellus savii*.

Northern bat *Vespertilio nilssoni*.

PARTI-COLOURED BAT

ORDER	Chiroptera
FAMILY	Vespertilionidae
GENUS	*Vespertilio*
SPECIES	*V. murinus*

Description: larger than Northern bat (head and body 55–63mm (2½in)) and whiter underparts, so appearing more distinctly bi-coloured. Mainly eastern Europe and southern Scandinavia, southwest and eastern England, Shetlands.

Parti-colored bat *Vespertilio murinus*.

MOUNTAIN, VARYING OR BLUE HARE

ORDER	Lagomorpha
FAMILY	Leporidae
GENUS	*Lepus*
SPECIES	*L. timidus*

Description: stockier than Brown hare with larger head, shorter ears and tail, and longer legs. In summer and autumn woolly fur brown with a grey 'blue' tint, underparts and tail white. Three annual moults. Fur

Mountain hare in summer coat.

Mountain, Varying or Blue hare
Lepus timidus.

usually turns white in winter but tips of ears remain black and outer half of ear below black tip remains brown. Amount of white in winter coat varies. In far north coat remains white throughout year while Irish race remains brown throughout year. The occurrence of a white pelage controlled by temperature and light intensity. Size variable. Head and body length 46–61cm (18–24in), tail 4·5–8cm (1½–3in), weight up to 5kg (10lb).

Range: whole northern part of Eurasia and in European Alps. Introduced to Faeroes. In Britain, originally confined to Scottish Highlands, introduced to southern Scotland, northern England and Wales.

Habitat: lives mainly above line of cultivation in open and wooded habitats. In mountainous country may descend to lower ground in winter especially to browse woodlands.

Life history: breeds February to July. Gestation about 50 days. Up to three litters of usually 2–3 young a year. Young never breed until year after birth. 10-year cycle of abundance.

Feeding: heather, willow, sedges and grasses. In winter bark, twigs, lichens and especially heather. Refection practised.

Habits: crepuscular and nocturnal. Spends day in form in long grass, in cavity amongst rocks or in short, simple burrow. More sociable than Brown hare especially in winter in favourable habitat. Voice a scream similar to brown hare. Record of intermittent feeble neighing sound during copulation. Sometimes a hiss if disturbed. Young preyed on by Wolf, fox, Glutton, Stoat and Wild cat, adults by Golden eagle, Buzzard, Eagle owl, Snowy owl, Gyrfalcon.

MARMOT

ORDER	Rodentia
FAMILY	Sciuridae
GENUS	*Marmota*
SPECIES	*M. marmota*

Description: heavily-built ground squirrel with short legs, short tail, broad rounded head and small ears. Fur reddish-yellow with patches of ash-grey on head, shoulders and rump, outer half of tail black. Head and body 50—57·5cm (20—23in), tail 13—16cm (5—6½in), weight 4—8kg (9—18lb).

Range: Swiss Alps, Tatra Mountains; introduced into Russian Carpathians.

Habitat: alpine pastures above tree-line.

Life history: breeds April. Gestation 6 weeks. One litter a year (perhaps one per two years) of 2—4 young which first emerge in July, not fully grown for 2 years, breed at 3 years (?). Longevity 20 years.

Feeding: eats grass, sedges, her-

Marmot *Marmota marmota*.

baceous plants, roots. No cheek pouches.

Habits: diurnal, sits on haunches to watch for predators. Warning whistle alerts colony, all scramble for burrows. Complicated burrow system, with tunnels down to 3m (10ft) and 10m (30ft) long, and with large resting chamber lined with dried grass, replaced before and after hibernation, which is in October to April. Prey, but rarely, of foxes and eagles.

NORWAY LEMMING

ORDER	Rodentia
FAMILY	Cricetidae
GENUS	*Lemmus*
SPECIES	*L. lemmus*

Norway lemming *Lemmus lemmus*.

Description: round-bodied, short legs, broad feet with hindfeet completely haired, stumpy tail, blunt muzzle, small eyes and small ears hidden in fur. Thick, long fur, yellow brown above, boldly patterned with blackish-brown streaks and patches, lighter below. Head and body length about 130mm (5in) with very short tail, weight 42–45g (under 2oz).

Range: tundra and mountains of Scandinavia, also northwest Russia.

Habitat: in summer moist stony ground, partly covered by sedges, willow shrubs and dwarf birch, in autumn move to drier areas. Always 750–1000m (2500–3300ft) above sea level.

Life history: gestation 20–22 days. Several litters a year with 4–8 young, possibly more, in summer, in nest of grass, fibres and moss. Breeding in winter under snow has been recorded, and is now believed to be one of main causes of cyclic population explosions. Period of lactation about 20 days. Young sexually mature soon after weaning and can breed from 4–5 weeks.

Feeding: grass roots, sedges, moss, lichens, fungi. Records of eating carrion.

Habits: usually nocturnal but also active by day, especially when numbers high. In summer burrows just beneath surface, in winter tunnels under snow, protected from cold and from some enemies, making rounded nests of grass exposed to view when snow melts. Gregarious, often quarrelsome especially when numbers high. When alarmed, individuals raise themselves on hindquarters, squeaking and grunting and giving general alarm. Do not wander far from burrows. Subject to cyclic rises in populations, when excess numbers move down into valleys and spread out, eventually some reaching sea and drowning. Will swim reluctantly across river if water calm and can see other bank. Heavily preyed upon by Arctic fox, Stoat, Weasel, buzzards, skuas, Snowy owl and members of crow family.

Special features: traditional stories of migrations in columns to commit mass-suicide in rivers and sea unfounded. Migration outward from normal habitat, under pressure of excess population, does take place but is not directional.

NEHRING'S SNOW VOLE

ORDER	Rodentia
FAMILY	Microtidae
GENUS	*Dolomys*
SPECIES	*D. milleri*
	(=*D. bogdanovi*)

Description: chinchilla-like, with long silky fur, blue-grey on upper-parts, white underparts. Otherwise, external features as in typical voles, except ear prominent above fur but not large. Small thumb bears flattened nail, remaining toes have claws. Head and body 99–148mm (4–6in), tail 74–119mm (3–4¾in) weight 150–280g (5¼–10oz).

Range: first discovered 1922, confined to mountains of Yugoslavia at 680–2100m (2100–6300ft).

Habitat: rocky slopes, grassland or wooded slopes.

Life history: two litters a year, April and July, of 2–3 young, after a month's gestation.

Feeding: eats grasses and stores grass.

Habits: mainly nocturnal. Nests in rock crevices or in burrows under large stones.

Nehring's snow vole *Dolomys milleri*.

FATIO'S PINE OR ROOT VOLE

ORDER	Rodentia
FAMILY	Microtidae
GENUS	*Pitymys*
SPECIES	*P. incertus*
	(=*P. multiplex*)

Description: indistinguishable from Pine vole *P. subterraneus* (p. 186) except for more yellowish fur and number of chromosomes (2n=48 as compared with 2n=54). Also, lives in Swiss Alps.

167

Pitymys tatricus: from Tatra Mountains of Czechoslovakia, at 1300–2300m (4000–7000ft), resembles the Pine vole *P. subterraneus* except in having a slightly larger size and in its rusty-coloured fur. It also has litters of 2–3 young, but its chromosome number is 2n=32 against 2n=54 of *P. subterraneus*.

Pitymys bavaricus: known only since 1962, from one locality in a valley in Bavaria at 730m (2200ft), may prove to be a local race of *P. tatricus* or *P. incertus*.

SNOW OR ALPINE VOLE

ORDER	Rodentia
FAMILY	Microtidae
GENUS	*Microtus*
SPECIES	*M. nivalis*

Description: large light grey vole with long whiskers and white tail, underparts white. Head and body 117–140mm (4½–5½in), tail 50–75mm (2–3in), weight 38–50g (1⅓–2oz).

Range: most mountain ranges of central and southern Europe; lowlands in southern France, 1600–2600m (5000–8000ft).

Habitat: stony meadows, rocky slopes, open woodlands, up to snow-line, especially where sunny.

Life history: much as in Common vole.

Feeding: food includes various grasses, herbaceous plants, twigs of bilberry.

Habits: seen by day in sunny weather, frequently basks on a grass tussock (unusual in rodents). Runs high on legs, tail erect. Jumps, climbs, swims well. Digs tunnel system with several openings, with nesting and storage chambers. Nest of dry grass and bents. Voice a single high-pitched note; chattering in breeding season.

Snow or Alpine vole *Microtus nivalis*.

GUENTHER'S OR MEDITERRANEAN VOLE

ORDER	Rodentia
FAMILY	Microtidae
GENUS	*Microtus*
SPECIES	*M. guentheri*

Description: similar to, and slightly larger than, Common vole

M. arvalis (p. 60) but has shorter tail (about $\frac{1}{4}$ length of head and body). Habitat and behaviour also similar.

Range: Greece and European Turkey; also Asia Minor to Israel and coast of Cyrenaica, in Libya.

Guenther's or Mediterranean vole *Microtus guentheri*.

CABRERA'S VOLE

ORDER	Rodentia
FAMILY	Microtidae
GENUS	*Microtus*
SPECIES	*M. cabrerae*

Description: known from a few museum specimens only, collected in various parts of Spain. Fur yellowish-brown above, yellowish below. Has very long guard hairs, especially on rump.

MOUFLON

ORDER	Artiodactyla
FAMILY	Bovidae
GENUS	*Ovis*
SPECIES	*O. musimon*

Description: wild sheep with short, non-fleecy coat, rams with large curving horns, ewes with small horns or none. Coat reddish-brown with dark markings, white lower legs and white patch on each flank. Head and body 110–130cm (43–51in), tail 3·5–6cm ($1\frac{1}{2}$–$2\frac{1}{2}$in), height at shoulder 65–75cm (26–30in), weight 25–50kg (55–110lb).

Range: Corsica, Sardinia, introduced France, Italy, Germany, Switzerland, Austria, Hungary, Czechoslovakia, Poland, Yugoslavia, USSR.

Habitat: woods on mountains,

Marks left on tree bark by Mouflon.

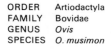

169

often also above tree-line. Can adapt to lowland woods or grasslands.

Life history: gestation 150 days.

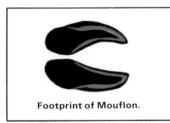

Footprint of Mouflon.

Mouflon *Ovis musimon*.

1—3 lambs born usually April. Sexual maturity at 18 months. Longevity 20 years.

Feeding: morning and evening especially, on grasses, herbaceous plants, sedges, heaths, leaves of bushes, shrubs.

Habits: in summer rams in groups apart from ewes and young. Autumn, rams fight for mastery of harems.

IBEX OR WILD GOAT

ORDER	Artiodactyla
FAMILY	Bovidae
GENUS	*Capra*
SPECIES	*C. hircus*

Description: Wild goat, grey with darker areas and black line along lower flanks, white underside. Horns long, heavy, curved, marked with

Male Ibex *Capra hircus*.

rings, less robust in females. 'Beard' on underside of head. Head and body 130–145cm (51–57in), tail 12–15cm (5–6in), height at shoulder 65–85cm (26–34in), weight 75–120kg (165–265lb), female 50–55kg (110–120lb).

Range: Spain, Alps, introduced Bavaria, Yugoslavia.

Habitat: Alpine meadows, steep crags, 1300–3300m (4000–10,000ft).

Life history: rut in December–January, gestation 150–180 days, kids born May–June, usually one, sometimes twins.

Feeding: shrubs, heather, grass, sedges, lichens (especially in winter).

Habits: males form own groups apart from females and young and usually occupy higher ground. Flocks of both sexes rest at higher altitudes by day, coming down to

Female Ibex.

feed by night. Voice a hiss or whistle. Enemy, where present, Wolf.

Special features: nomenclature of wild goats in Europe confused. Some zoologists regard Ibex and wild (feral) goats as one species (*Capra hircus*), others differentiate between *C. ibex* and *C. hircus* and yet others treat each separate population of Ibexes as a distinct species or at least a subspecies. Domestic goat is descended from wild Ibex and interbreeds freely with it. This has been going on for over a thousand years, during which man has also moved the true wild Ibexes from place to place.

CHAMOIS

ORDER	Artiodactyla
FAMILY	Bovidae
GENUS	*Rupicapra*
SPECIES	*R. rupicapra*

Description: goat-like, distinguished by short vertical horns, in both sexes, with backward-curving tips. Coat dark-brown (winter) with white markings on head and throat, and white tail patch, summer coat lighter with dark band on lower flanks. Underside pale buff. Head and body 110–130cm (43–51in), tail 3–4cm (1½in), height at shoulder 70–80cm (28–32in), weight 30–59kg (66–130lb). Female lighter.

Range: mountains of southern

Chamois *Rupicapra rupicapra*.

Europe; also Caucasus and Asia Minor.

Habitat: wooded slopes, also above tree-line.

Life history: rut in October to December, gestation 153–180 days, lambs born April–June.

Feeding: grazer and browser, grasses, herbaceous plants, lichens, foliage of shrubs and trees (including conifers).

Winter coat of Chamois.

Habits: diurnal, moves between feeding and resting places. Males solitary at rut, later join herds of females and young which then coalesce to herds of several hundred.

Special features: remarkably sure-footed; will leap across crevices up to 6m (20ft) wide and land accurately on a rock surface 0·3m (1ft) in diameter.

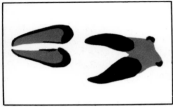

Footprint of Chamois.

WETLANDS

Unlike most other habitats described in this book, wetlands do not occur as a single zone or belt running across Europe. Their distribution is scattered and they include habitats associated with marshes, streams, rivers and lakes. Wetlands provide various types of habitat. Obviously the basic characteristic in all of them is the presence of water, but the effect of this presence varies from place to place. At one extreme, for example, a river may flow through a mixed woodland habitat which is unaffected except at a narrow zone running along the river bank. At the other extreme, a poorly drained area such as a marsh or bog will be greatly affected by the presence of water and support only aquatic life.

The word fen refers to a wetland area where vegetation grows on peat, which has developed in the presence of moving, mineral-rich water. It is the presence of peat that distinguishes fen from marsh. The type of vegetation found in fen depends on two factors: the extent to which terrestrialization has taken place, that is the extent to which silting has produced relatively dry areas within the fen, and whether the water moves above or below the surface of the peat. If the water moves below the surface, the vegetation is in the nature of a turf of floating and weakly rooted plants including certain mosses, sedges, king cups, the bog bean, broad-leaved cotton grass and marsh bedstraw. However, when water flows on the surface of the peat, even for part of the year, the only plants that survive are those that are well rooted and resist being washed away: such plants include the common reed, reed maces and reed-grass.

The division of fens into turf and reed fens implied by the foregoing descriptions is, in fact, an over-simplification. The fens with the most varied floras are those that contain a mixture of turf and reed plants and in reality there is a gradation between the two types of fen. Any change in the water level may alter reed fen to turf fen and vice versa. The fen may even become colonized by woody plants if the water level drops sufficiently low and sallow buckthorn and alder are often found. When this woody cover is complete, the vegetation is referred to as carr.

Perhaps more than any other European habitat, wetlands have

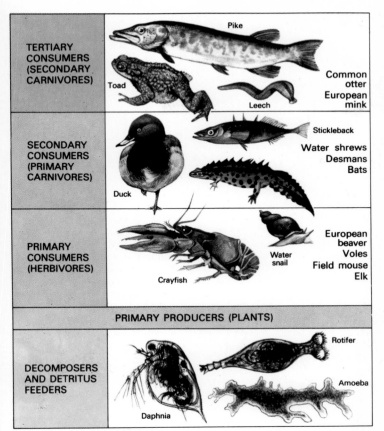

TERTIARY CONSUMERS (SECONDARY CARNIVORES)	Pike Toad Leech	Common otter European mink
SECONDARY CONSUMERS (PRIMARY CARNIVORES)	Duck Stickleback	Water shrews Desmans Bats
PRIMARY CONSUMERS (HERBIVORES)	Crayfish Water snail	European beaver Voles Field mouse Elk
PRIMARY PRODUCERS (PLANTS)		
DECOMPOSERS AND DETRITUS FEEDERS	Daphnia Rotifer Amoeba	

changed during the past centuries as a result of the influence of man. Fens, drained and cleared of woodland, provide rich agricultural land which is used for grazing and numerous arable crops, as well as for fruit and bulbs. There is evidence that drainage ditches or dykes were cut in the East Anglian region of Britain during the Roman occupation.

There is no doubt that the draining of wetlands has been the major method by which man has changed this habitat; however, the removal of peat for fuel has also been significant. Man has also had a direct effect on the fenland vegetation simply by cropping it for kindling, basket-making, thatch and hay. The beds of saw sedge in particular have been reduced because of the value of this species for thatching. Finally, man, by introducing the Coypu from South America in 1929 has reduced areas of reed beds, and prevented the establishment of carr. The Coypu is bred for its valuable pelt, but individuals have escaped and

become naturalized in wetlands where they feed on reeds and plants which constitute the peat mat, thus preventing the growth of a strong base on which tussocks of grass and seedlings can establish themselves.

Feeding relationships. With the strictures of terrestrial life and its problems of desiccation and respiration removed, invertebrate life teems in wetlands. These form the basis of one of the most complex food webs in nature.

Most of the freshwater fish such as Roach, Tench, Stickleback and Bream feed directly on these invertebrates as do many birds, particularly dippers, ducks, geese and swans. There are also vast numbers of predatory invertebrates which are a highly important part of the secondary consumer network. Frogs and

newts are more specialized, preying mainly on worms and insect larvae though they will take molluscs and crustacea. Where common, the Water spider is also an important predator, but in water arachnids are most ubiquitously represented by mites, which fill an amazing diversity of niches ranging from herbivore to parasite. It is hardly surprising, therefore, that some insectivorous mammals have invaded aquatic conditions to take advantage of this bonanza. Shrews and desmans take mainly worms, insects and crustaceans and bats the winged insect adults.

Herbivorous animals such as beavers, voles, Elks and mice, have little competition and abound, in contrast to the secondary carnivores, the otter and mink, which must compete with the fish-eating birds, reptiles and fish.

EUROPEAN WATER SHREW

ORDER	Insectivora
FAMILY	Soricidae
GENUS	*Neomys*
SPECIES	*N. fodiens*

Description: stout body, snout short and broad, small eyes blue, ears white, almost entirely concealed beneath fur and tuft of white hairs above each eye. Broad, brown feet, digits fringed with stiff hairs (making feet paddle-like), tail tapering, flattened from side to side with double fringe of strong, silvery-grey hairs along underside, constituting a 'keel' and making it more efficient as a rudder. Fine, dense fur, longer in winter, slaty black to dark brown on

Water shrew *Neomys fodiens*.

upperparts and light ash grey or dirty white on underparts, colours sharply separated. Sometimes underparts nearly as dark as upperparts. Teeth have coloured tips like those of other shrews but points of incisors more hooked. Head and body length: 76–96mm (3–3¾in), tail 52–72mm (2–2¾in)' hind foot usually exceeds 19mm (¾in), weight about 12–18g (½oz), lowest in winter.

Range: throughout Europe except for Mediterranean lowlands; north to Arctic Ocean. In Asia north to about Arctic Circle, east to Pacific coast and Sakhalin. Up to 1800m (6000ft).

Habitat: marshes, watercress beds, banks of streams with good ground cover, also woodland and scrub miles from any water. In Poland extends into conifer and deciduous woods.

Life history: breeding season April to September. Gestation 24 days. Up to at least 3 litters a year of 5–8 blind, naked young each weighing just over 1g. Eyes open 22 days. Weaning at 4 weeks. Independent at 5 or 6 weeks. Some females breed in year of birth.

Feeding: whirligig beetles, water gnats, caddis-worms and other aquatic larvae. Also water snails, worms, small crustaceans, frogs, small fishes and carrion. Secretion from submaxillary glands poisonous, lethal even to small rodents.

Habits: in water very buoyant, swimming with head slightly above surface, with alternate strokes of

The Water shrew is able to hunt underwater for short periods.

limbs and laterally undulating movements of body. Can walk on bottom and takes distinct leaps out of water presumably after flying insects. On land sometimes has bounding gait. Short excursions into water then returns to land to groom fur. Dries fur by squeezing through tight-fitting tunnels. Under water fur carries good deal of air trapped in it giving body silvery appearance, like 'animated air bubble'. Shallow burrows in bank for sleeping quarters, farther in for nursery chamber, lined with moss and fine roots, or a round nest of woven grass or leaves. No hibernation. Can be seen in winter pursuing prey beneath ice. Solitary with overlapping home ranges. Voice a shrill cricket-like chirp near upper limits of human ear. Chief enemies owls, but also taken by predatory mammals which prey on Common shrews, and larger predatory fishes.

MEDITERRANEAN OR MILLER'S WATER SHREW

Mediterranean or Miller's water shrew *Neomys anomalus*.

ORDER	Insectivora
FAMILY	Soricidae
GENUS	*Neomys*
SPECIES	*N. anomalus*

Description: similar to *N. fodiens* but often smaller and underparts always white. Also, no marked keel of stiff hairs on underside of tail and fringe on hindfeet less obvious. Head and body 64–88mm ($2\frac{1}{2}$–$3\frac{1}{2}$in), tail 42–64mm ($1\frac{2}{3}$–$2\frac{1}{2}$in), weight 7·5–16g ($\frac{1}{4}$–$\frac{1}{2}$oz) (Poland: *N. anomalus* much smaller than *N. fodiens*; in southern parts of range *N. anomalus* as big as *N. fodiens*).

Range: lives in marshes and wet grassland and near streams: a) in mountains of central and N.W. Spain, Pyrenees, Alps, Calabria, Balkans; b) forest-steppes in Poland (Bialowieza); c) steppes in southern Russia and Crimea.

Habits and life history: similar to those of *N. fodiens*.

PYRENEAN DESMAN

ORDER	Insectivora
FAMILY	Talpidae
GENUS	*Galemys*
SPECIES	*G. pyrenaicus*

Description: shrew-like relative of moles, with a long spatulate snout, short neck, small eyes and ears and relatively large, webbed hindfeet, all feet ringed with stiff hairs. Tail long, laterally compressed, fringed with

Pyrenean desman *Galemys pyrenaicus*.

stiff hairs. Nostrils on upper side of snout, valved. Upperparts dark brown, underside silvery-white with yellowish patch on breast. Fur consists of dense underfur and long guard hairs. Head and body 110–135mm (4½–5½in), tail 130–155mm (5–6in), weight 50–80g (2–3oz).

Range: northern Spain and Portugal, French Pyrenees.

Habitat: mountain streams, marshes, wet meadows.

Life history: breeds January–February, litter of (usually) 4 born March–July.

Feeding: mainly aquatic invertebrates, taken almost exclusively on river bed, desman moving like a mole in soft soil.

Habits: mostly nocturnal, solitary but high density (eg 79 individuals in 1km (⅝mi) stretch of river). Swims with hindfeet. Shelters in cavities between stones and tree roots on river banks (does not make burrows).

RUSSIAN DESMAN

ORDER	Insectivora
FAMILY	Talpidae
GENUS	*Desmana*
SPECIES	*D. moschata*

Description: similar in form and habits to Pyrenean desman but larger, 44cm (17in) long, with strong musky odour from glands situated

under base of tail. Hunted for its fur.

Range: southern Russia (Don and Volga basins).

DAUBENTON'S OR WATER BAT

ORDER	Chiroptera
FAMILY	Vespertilionidae
GENUS	*Myotis*
SPECIES	*M. daubentoni*

Description: head and body 50mm (2in), tail 32mm (1¼in), forearm 32mm (1¼in), wingspan 250mm (10in). Ear short but longer than broad, tragus slender, short. Fur greyish red-brown above, dull white below. Leaves roost soon after sunset, flies low over standing or slow-moving water hawking gnats and other aquatic insects. Europe except extreme north, Balkans, much of Italy.

Daubenton's or Water bat *Myotis daubentoni.*

LONG-FINGERED BAT

ORDER	Chiroptera
FAMILY	Vespertilionidae
GENUS	*Myotis*
SPECIES	*M. capaccinii*

Description: very like Daubenton's bat but hindlegs and adjacent membranes noticeably hairy. Southern Europe.

Long-fingered bat *Myotis capaccinii.*

POND BAT

ORDER	Chiroptera
FAMILY	Vespertilionidae
GENUS	*Myotis*
SPECIES	*M. dasycneme*

Description: very like Daubenton's bat but larger (head and body 57—61mm (2¼in), tail 46—51mm (2in), forearm 43—47mm (1¾in), weight up to 15—19·5g (⁵⁄₇oz)). Central Europe, Low Countries and Germany eastwards to Urals.

Pond bat *Myotis dasycneme.*

European beaver
Castor fiber.

EUROPEAN BEAVER

ORDER	Rodentia
FAMILY	Castoridae
GENUS	*Castor*
SPECIES	*C. fiber*

Description: largest European rodent, highly adapted for aquatic life. Stout-bodied, muzzle blunt, ears small, tail scaly, broad, flat, used as paddle, legs short, hindfeet webbed, front toes clawed for digging. Brown coat with dense underfur and sleek, water-repellent outer covering of guard hairs, southern forms lighter in colour than northern. Head and body length up to 90cm (35½in), tail up to 38cm (15in), weight 14–34kg (30–75lb). Heavier forms on Rhône, lightest in Scandinavia.

Range: greatly reduced in numbers by exploitation for fur. Once widespread over Europe and northern half of Asia, now one of rarest mammals

in small numbers in Scandinavia, Rhône and Elbe valleys, and European Russia.

Habitat: rivers and lakes in wooded country.

Life history: mate in January to February, gestation 60–128 days. One litter a year, usually 2–4 young, born in burrow or lodge with coat of soft fur and eyes open. Weaning complete at 6 weeks. Remain with parents for first winter, sometimes second. Mature 2–3 years.

Feeding: bark, especially of aspen and willow, from branches of trees they have felled. In summer wide variety of green food, mostly aquatic plants and thistles. Twigs and branches stored near burrow or lodge for winter use eaten mainly by youngsters; older beavers live on their fat and eat little during winter.

Habits: mainly nocturnal, very shy and wary, live in water most of time. Normally pair for life, living in colonies — family unit of up to 12 — usually in burrows in river bank with underwater entrance, but, now rarely, they also build elaborate dams and a lodge. Main dam, of branches, mud and stones, causes overflow of river banks, forming beaver-pond. In centre of pond, often by clump of young trees, lodge is built of sticks and mud, with underwater entrances, central chamber above water-level and a ventilating chimney from chamber to top of lodge. Walks clumsily but skilful swimmer and diver, often slaps water with tail as it dives, presumably as alarm. Usually silent animal. Adults preyed on only by larger carnivores such as Brown bear; young taken by Mink and larger birds of prey.

Tree showing signs of gnawing by a beaver.

Special features: extermination of Beaver over most of its former range due partly to its valuable fur, but also for glandular secretion, used to mark territories, known as castoreum and used as a cure-all in 16th and 17th centuries. Analysis shows castoreum contains salicylic acid, one of ingredients of aspirin.

Section through a beaver dam showing underwater entrance.

Water vole *Arvicola terrestris*.

WATER VOLE

ORDER	Rodentia
FAMILY	Microtidae
GENUS	*Arvicola*
SPECIES	*A. amphibius*

Description: large vole with long, thick, glossy fur, upperparts blackish-grey or warm reddish-brown sprinkled with grey. Underparts yellowish-grey. Short thick head and chubby face with rounded muzzle. Limbs relatively short, small eyes, small brown ears scarcely projecting beyond fur. Feet naked, pale pink on underside with 5 rounded pads and stiff hairs on upper surface. Prominent scent glands on flanks. Females slightly smaller than males and more greyish-brown. Considerable regional variation in size in Europe. In central Europe and especially in Alps, smaller with forwardly projecting incisors. Large form in Britain and northern Europe.

Head and body length: 190–215mm (7½–8½in). Tail c. 114mm (4½in). Weight varies from 120–180g (3¾–5¾oz) in winter to almost double in summer.

Range: widespread Palearctic species from tundra to wooded steppe zone from western Europe to central Siberia.

Habitat: In Britain and northern Europe lives in and near slow-flowing rivers and lakes with well-vegetated banks. In Scottish highlands ascends burns up to about 600m (2000ft). In central Europe often lives in grasslands far from water, digging extensive tunnels like those of mole.

Life history: breeds April to October. Gestation 21 or 22 days. Post-partum conception can occur usually in first part of season. Young born underground in burrow or above ground in reed beds etc. Litter size 2–7 (usually 5) born naked and blind. Young from earlier litters may breed in their first year. Number of litters in year not known for certain. Longevity little more than 1 year. Older individuals are driven out of territories by younger voles and more readily fall victim to predators.

Feeding: predominantly on green waterside vegetation. Small amount of animal food. Habit of sitting up and holding food with forepaws. Some damage by barking trees and eating twigs. Stores food when scarce and difficult to find. Food: green vegetation especially flotegrass, reed and reed-grass, nuts, beechmast, acorns, underground stems of horsetails stored; in winter roots (including cultivated root-crops) and rhizomes.

Habits: sleeps in burrows in banks. Breeding nest thick-walled and globular made of reeds and grasses in excavated chamber under bank, in reed-bed, in hollow willow or even in disused bird's nest. Opinions differ on circadian rhythm: 1) activity begins about 4 (in the morning) continuing fairly active to 4 (in the afternoon), rising to peak at 9 (in the evening), with little activity at night; 2) main activity at dusk and little during day; 3) 4-hourly rhythm throughout day and night, with feeding periods of about an hour alternating with periods of rest or random movement.

Voice a chattering especially when fighting intruders in spring.

Preyed upon especially by Mink, of which it probably forms dominant food, and by Otters. Also by herons, owls, Stoats, Weasels, rats, pike, eels, large trout.

Populations: considerable population fluctuations, much greater on Continent than in British Isles.

Special features: home range of resident animals not more than 180m (200 yards) long. Males fight intruders fiercely especially in spring. Home range marked by section of flank glands conveyed to ground by hind-feet. Steady swimmer, at 4kph (2½–3mph). Less skilful in swimming than in diving. Does damage on Continent and in Fenland by burrowing into banks of dykes and eating root crops and potatoes. Farther east carries bacillus of *Tularaemia*.

Senses: sight: very short-sighted. One can bring one's face to within a foot of Water vole's face, looking straight into its eye and vole will continue feeding. Slightest sound or movement causes it to dive under water again.

Water vole with young.

EUROPEAN PINE VOLE

ORDER	Rodentia
FAMILY	Microtidae
GENUS	*Pitymys*
SPECIES	*P. subterraneus*

Description: typical vole, mouse-like with small eyes, ears hidden in fur, snout blunt. Dark brown, slightly lighter on underside. Head and body 75–106mm (3–4in), tail 25·5–39mm (1–1½in), weight 12·5–23·5g (½–1oz).

Range: western France to River Don, north to about latitude 52°N, southwards nearly to Mediterranean region.

Habitat: damp meadows, open woodlands, rarely in coniferous woods, in places at high altitude.

Life history: long breeding season with up to 9 litters a year, each of 2–3 young (female has only two teats).

Feeding: eats underground parts of plants.

Habits: makes extensive burrows, with tunnels just under surface to 31cm (1ft) down, and with nesting and storage chambers. Sociable. Lives much of its life underground. Voice includes twittering and squeaking; hisses when alarmed.

European pine vole *Pitymys subterraneus*.

SAVI'S PINE OR MEDITERRANEAN ROOT VOLE

ORDER	Rodentia
FAMILY	Microtidae
GENUS	*Pitymys*
SPECIES	*P. savii*

Description: closely resembles Pine vole *Pitymys subterraneus* except that fur is reddish-brown and range includes N.W. Iberia, southern

France, most of Italy, Sicily, southern parts of Yugoslavia and Greece.

Mediterranean pine or Iberian root vole *Pitymys duodecimostatus*.

MEDITERRANEAN PINE OR IBERIAN ROOT VOLE

ORDER	Rodentia
FAMILY	Microtidae
GENUS	*Pitymys*
SPECIES	*P. duodecimostatus*

Description: closely resembles Mediterranean root vole *P. savii* but very slightly larger, more reddish fur. Habitat similar. Range includes most of Portugal and Spain and extreme south of France.

FIELD OR SHORT-TAILED VOLE

ORDER	Rodentia
FAMILY	Muridae
GENUS	*Microtus*
SPECIES	*M. agrestis*

Description: stumpy body, blunt oval head, short round ears just protruding from fur, short, rather stiff tail. Hindfeet have six pads on undersurface. Upperparts yellowish-brown to dark brown, underside

Short-tailed vole *Microtus agrestis*.

greyish-white. Buff and sandy forms not uncommon. Head and body length 88–114mm (3½–4½in), tail 31–46mm (1¼–1¾in), weight variable 20–40g (⅔–1⅓oz).

Range: across Europe from Arctic coast south to Pyrenees and Alps, eastwards to River Yenisei and Lake Baikal.

Habitat: typically meadows and damp pastures but also open woodlands among bracken, gardens, orchards and plantations. Needs fairly dense ground cover.

Life history: breeding season March to October in centre of range, but sometimes to December. Gestation 21 days. Several litters a year with usually 3–6 naked and blind young. Weaned 14–18 days, sexually mature 3 weeks, mate at 6 weeks. Very few survive second winter.

Feeding: almost entirely herbivorous, feeding especially on stems and leaves of grasses, rushes and sedges. In winter roots, rhizomes and bark. Also eats insects and carrion. Much damage to orchards and plantations. Food stored in burrows.

Habits: shallow underground burrows connect with network of runs above ground through grass and herbage with occasional bolt holes. Alternating periods of 2–3 hours of activity and 2–3 hours sleep throughout 24 hours, those at night slightly longer. Nest made beside tuft of grass along run or under log. Usually roofed with dome of grass blades split longitudinally and plaited and felted. Very difficult to see. Runs fast, swims well but seldom climbs. Loud chattering voice. Preyed upon particularly by owls, Kestrel, Buzzard, foxes and Weasels.

Populations: one of most abundant and widespread voles. High reproductive potential. Sometimes increases to plague proportions causing widespread damage to vegetation and crops. Peak every four years.

ROOT VOLE

ORDER	Rodentia
FAMILY	Microtidae
GENUS	*Microtus*
SPECIES	*M. ratticeps*

Description: similar to Common vole but darker and with relatively longer tail. Fur dark brown, dirty white on underparts. Head and body 118–148mm (4¾–6in), tail 40–64mm (1½–2½in), weight 24–62g (1–2oz).

Range: Scandinavia and Finland, south of Baltic from the line Elbe to Rumania and eastwards to Asia. Also Alaska and parts of Canada.

Habitat: marshes, wet grasslands, reed beds.

Habits: resembles Field vole *M. agrestis* in life-history, behaviour and ecology but burrows more.

Root vole *Microtus ratticeps*.

STRIPED FIELD MOUSE

ORDER	Rodentia
FAMILY	Muridae
GENUS	*Apodemus*
SPECIES	*A. agrarius*

Description: reddish-brown mouse with white underparts, pink feet, large ears and long tail. Distinguished by black stripe from back of head to base of tail. Head and body 97—122mm (4—5in), tail 66—68mm (2½in), weight 16—25g (½—1oz).

Range: eastern Europe south of latitude 60°N to Bulgaria, westwards across northern Germany to Denmark, also from Rumania westwards into Hungary.

Habitat: damp areas of parkland, open woods, steppes, grassland and arable land.

Life history: gestation 21—22 days, several litters a year of 5—7 young.

Habits: habits similar to those of Wood mouse *A. sylvaticus* but less agile and climbs less. In winter enters stables and barns. Builds nest chambers and stores food underground.

Striped field mouse *Apodemus agrarius*.

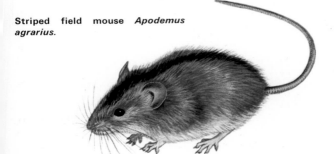

European mink *Mustela lutreola*.

EUROPEAN MINK

ORDER	Carnivora
FAMILY	Mustelidae
GENUS	*Mustela*
SPECIES	*M. lutreola*

Description: long, slender body slung low, ears short, set close together, bushy tail, short legs, toes partly webbed. Uniformly deep brown fur. Lower lip, and usually upper lip, spotted with white. Head and body length 35–40cm (14–16in), tail 13–14cm (5in), weight 550–800g (1¼–2lb).

Range: European Russia, Finland, eastern and central Europe, possibly France.

Habitat: by streams, rivers and lakes especially in or near woods, also marshes.

Life history: mating February to March, usually 4–5 young in litter born April to June, after a gestation period of 45–70 days.

Feeding: particularly on small rodents, especially Water voles, but frogs, newts, ducks, crayfish and molluscs also taken.

Habits: nocturnal and solitary. Dens in clefts of rocks or in hole in bank, between tree roots, in hollow trees or in burrow excavated by itself. Sometimes nests above ground in dense reed beds. Piping noises when alarmed.

Special features: a disappearing species in Europe but within last century has spread beyond Urals into western Siberia.

Common otter *Lutra lutra*.

COMMON OTTER

ORDER	Carnivora
FAMILY	Mustelidae
GENUS	*Lutra*
SPECIES	*L. lutra*

Description: fur of two kinds: fine, soft waterproof underfur of whitish-grey with brown tips, interspersed with longer and thicker glossy guard hairs. Whole body appears a rich brown. Hairs on cheeks, throat and underparts light brown to silvery grey. Colour varies with season, being richer and darker brown in winter. Occasional cream or white specimens recorded. Possibly autumn moult or continuous moulting throughout most of year. Long, lithe body, head broad and flat, face short, eyes black small but bright. Short, rounded, hairy ears do not project beyond fur. Legs short and powerful, all feet completely webbed. Five toes on each foot, those of forefeet have short pointed claws. Claws of hind feet more flattened and nail-like. Long, thick tapering tail used as rudder. Below base of tail pair of glands give off fetid fluid.

Total length about 1·2m (4ft) of which ⅓ is tail. Records from skins of 2·3m (7ft). Weight of full-grown male 9–12kg (20–25lb), occasionally exceeds 12·2kg (27lb). Records of 23kg (50lb) and almost 27kg (60lb).

Range: Europe, North Africa and most of Asia.

Habitat: lakes, rivers, streams and marshes, reed-beds, coastal waters. Travels overland up to 19km (12m) in a night, from pool to pool. Sometimes moves up to mountainous areas when fish migrate up to head waters to spawn.

Life history: little known about breeding. Young born at all times of year. Gestation 63 days but may be delayed implantation. 2–3 cubs in a litter, born blind but covered with fine, dark, downy fur. Eyes open at 35 days. Cubs remain in 'hover' or nursery nest for several weeks before being taken to water; probably do not leave mother until she is ready to breed again. Life span in captivity 23 years.

Feeding: essentially a fisher, bringing catch to bank to be consumed. Various fish, especially eels, frogs, newts, freshwater shrimps, occasionally wild ducks, moorhens. On land, Rabbits, rats, mice, voles, slugs, earthworms, beetles. Crayfish favourite food. Starts hunting about sunset. Favourite trick is to float with current downstream with forelegs pressed against sides and only upper head, eyes, ears and nostrils exposed above water. May do damage to trout and salmon hatcheries. In clear water eyes used for following quarry but in muddy or turbulent water whiskers used. Often in summer goes to coast, using cave as shelter, working shallow waters for flatfish, bass, crabs and mussels.

Food of the European otter: (1) fish, (2) crustaceans, (3) shellfish, (4) water birds, (5) amphibians and (6) small mammals.

Otters will commonly play and adopt postures unusual in wild mammals.

Habits: usually nocturnal, coming out at sunset. During day lies up in reed beds, burrows, drains, hollow trees. In summer may lie up in woods or caves by sea. Breeding holt a hole in a bank with entrance under water or it may be well away from water, lined with reeds, grass and moss. Can travel with speed on land. Will often play, including tobogganing down muddy slopes or over snow-covered or icy ground: two bounds and a slide often when going overland. Bitch and cubs swimming in line astern known to have given rise to stories of lake monsters. Senses

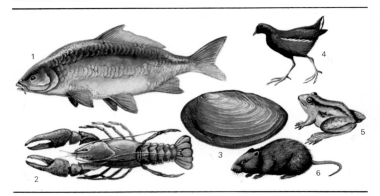

include stout whiskers set in glandular moustachial pad richly supplied with nerves – highly sensitive and doubtless pick up vibrations in water and guide otter to prey.

'Spraints' or droppings black when fresh, paler later.

Often silent for long periods. Flute-like whistle. Whickering of cubs. Long drawn-out moan, low pitched chortle of pleasure and hiss or high-pitched chatter of annoyance.

Elk *Alces alces*.

ELK

ORDER	Artiodactyla
FAMILY	Cervidae
GENUS	*Alces*
SPECIES	*A. alces*

Description: with closely related species of North America (*A. americana* = Moose), largest of deer family (Cervidae). Grey-brown to almost black, lighter on snout and legs. Broad, overhanging, down-curved muzzle, flap of hairy skin pendant from throat, male with large palmate (flat, with points) antlers. Head and body length in male 2–3m (6–9ft), tail 5cm (2in), height at shoulder 1·8–2·0m (5–6ft), weight 320–500kg (700–1100lb), female smaller 1·2–1·8m (4½–5ft), weight 275–375kg (600–820lb).

Range: Scandinavia, Finland, northern Russia, Poland.

Habitat: in summer, marshes especially where undergrowth of willow, birch and mountain ash; in winter, dryer, somewhat higher ground.

Life history: rut in September, bulls cease feeding, make a bugling roar, much fighting between them; each mates with several cows. Gestation 242–250 days. 1–3 calves (usually twins) born in May or June, are hidden in vegetation for first ten days, then follow mother until following spring, females sexually mature at 18 months, males a year later. Longevity 20 years.

Feeding: herbivorous, eating foliage of birch, willow, mountain ash, etc, also aquatic plants. Winter, feeds on shoots, also bark including that of conifers. Normally each individual keeps to small home range but may wander, even onto open steppe, out of sight of woods.

Habits: solitary in summer, forms small herds in winter under leadership of cow with calf. Most active at dawn and dusk, rests midday. Can trot at up to 56 kmph (35 mph). Swims and dives well, may remain

An Elk defending itself against a Wolf.

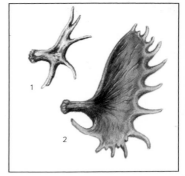

Antlers in immature (1) and mature (2) male Elk.

submerged for up to one minute. Often spends much of day in summer half-submerged. Migratory in winter in northern part of range. Voice a deep lowing but silent most of year, with bulls roaring (bugling) during rutting season. Cow and calf call to each other with plaintive cries. Calves preyed on by bear and wolf, adults by group of wolves.

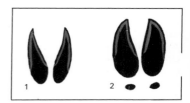

Footprints of young (1) and adult (2).

Populations: although long hunted and once extending to northern Germany, Elk numbers today are satisfactory. In northern Russia range is being extended. In southern Sweden, Elk near extinction in early 19th century but protection given 1826–1835 and numbers now 120,000 even where industry, agriculture, roads etc. have intruded into habitat.

SUBARCTIC

The subarctic, or taiga, lies south of the tundra and in Europe alone stretches for over 2,300km (1,400mi) from Scandinavia to the Ural Mountains. It takes in much of Norway, most of Sweden north of Stockholm, almost all Finland, and European Russia as far south as Leningrad.

Taiga is a Siberian word for an area in which conifers are a conspicuous element in the scenery, and where the ground tends to be barren and rocky. It has also been aptly called the forest tundra. The summers are short so that even where the ground is not virtually useless for cultivation only a limited selection of crops can be grown, such as barley, oats, potatoes and fodder hay. The taiga includes, in consequence, large uninhabited areas. Outside Europe it stretches eastwards and continues through northern Asia to the Pacific, and thus constitutes the largest continuous forest in the world.

During the Ice Age a tremendous volume of water was locked up as glaciers, the weight of which depressed the land beneath them. As the glaciers melted, water was released and the burden on the land was relieved. The outlines of the coast were correspondingly altered and there were other geographical changes. What is now subarctic Europe was, during the height of the Ice Age, submerged below the sea. With the retreat of the ice cap, and the melting of the glaciers, it became a vast archipelago which is reflected today in the topography, best seen in Finland, with its numerous lakes and marshes.

The proximity to the polar cap ensures that the mean annual temperature is low. Over much of subarctic Europe the summer temperatures range from 10–20 °C (50–68 °F), those of winter range from 0––20 °C (32––2 °F). The main isotherms, and therefore the southern boundary of the subarctic, show a sharp northward indentation over southern Norway due to the influence of the warmer waters of the Gulf Stream. One result of this is that the seas around the northern coast of Europe are never ice-bound. Nor is there any area of permafrost, where the ground is permanently frozen. This can be emphasized by the comparison between Norway in which the subarctic climate is as far north as latitude 70 °N and eastern Canada, where subarctic conditions occur south to latitude 52 °N.

The vegetation of the subarctic is typically coniferous but, due to the influence of the North Atlantic Drift, birch and willow as well as Scots pine spread far to the north in sheltered valleys, and birch forests may be found up to the edge of the tundra.

Feeding relationships. Low temperatures tend to prohibit much invertebrate life except in muddy coastal regions. Here filter- and detritus-feeding worms and bivalve molluscs provide abundant food supplies for waders. Geese, ducks and swans also find profitable feeding grounds on the mud flats and in the mouths of estuaries and fjords.

The basis of the food web in subarctic regions is large populations of small mammals, particu-

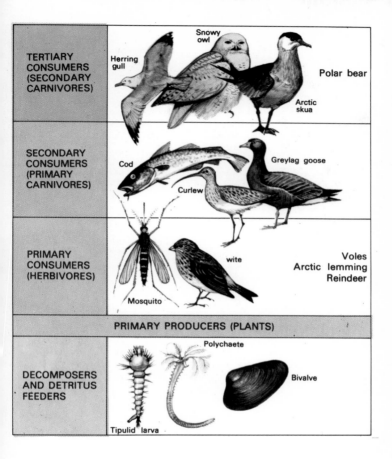

TERTIARY CONSUMERS (SECONDARY CARNIVORES)	Herring gull, Snowy owl, Polar bear, Arctic skua
SECONDARY CONSUMERS (PRIMARY CARNIVORES)	Cod, Curlew, Greylag goose
PRIMARY CONSUMERS (HERBIVORES)	Mosquito, wite, Voles, Arctic lemming, Reindeer
PRIMARY PRODUCERS (PLANTS)	
DECOMPOSERS AND DETRITUS FEEDERS	Tipulid larva, Polychaete, Bivalve

larly voles and lemmings, though finches and bunting species also serve as prey for Arctic foxes.

Insect life is abundant though consisting almost entirely of gnat, mosquito and midge swarms. Birds such as wagtails, warblers, martins and pipits take full advantage of these though there are few ground dwelling insects to support insectivorous mammals.

Apart from the Polar bear, the mammalian carnivores that do exist are strictly secondary carnivores and the Arctic fox is the only truly terrestrial predator. This small canid feeds mainly on vole and lemming species though it will take birds and insects if the opportunity arises. Competition is mainly from the owls and larger hawks, and the fox itself may fall prey to Rough-legged buzzards.

197

ARCTIC LEMMING

ORDER	Rodentia
FAMILY	Microtidae
GENUS	*Dicrostonyx*
SPECIES	*D. torquatus*

Description: lemming of tundra of northern Asia also extending into extreme N.E. of European Russia, 150mm (6in) long including stump of tail. Fur mainly reddish in summer with white collar, all white in winter.

Claws broad, especially on forefeet. Occasionally reaches Spitzbergen on ice-floes.

Arctic lemming *Dicrostonyx torquatus* in summer (1) and winter (2) coat.

RUDDY OR NORTHERN RED-BACKED VOLE

ORDER	Rodentia
FAMILY	Microtidae
GENUS	*Clethrionomys*
SPECIES	*C. rutilus*

Description: resembles Bank vole (p. 111) but reddish-brown upperparts, cream underside and very

Ruddy or northern red-backed vole *Clethrionomys rutilis*.

short tail. Head and body 100mm (4in), tail 25mm (1in), weight 15–40g (3/5–1½oz).

Range: northern Scandinavia, most of Finland, northern Russia.

LARGE-TOOTHED RED-BACKED OR GREY-SIDED VOLE

Description: resembles Bank vole (p. 111) in form and life-history. Reddish-brown on back and head, flanks and underside grey. Head and body 110–130mm (4½–5in), tail 28–40mm (1–1¾in), weight 18–19g (⅔oz).

Large-toothed red-backed vole *Clethrionomys rufocanus*.

Habitat: pine and birch zones.

Habits: similar to those of bank vole; makes nests between tree roots and stones. Enters houses.

ORDER	Rodentia
FAMILY	Microtidae
GENUS	*Clethrionomys*
SPECIES	*C. rufocanus*

Range: northern to central Scandinavia.

Habits: similar to those of Bank vole; makes nests between tree roots and stones. Enters houses.

Special features: has larger teeth than Bank vole, perhaps correlated with eating coarse heath vegetation.

ARCTIC FOX

ORDER	Carnivora
FAMILY	Canidae
GENUS	*Alopex*
SPECIES	*A. lagopus*

Description: smaller than Red fox with shorter muzzle, smaller ears, less bushy tail and soles covered with fur. Two colour phases: a) coat grey to greyish-brown, white below, in summer, pure white with creamy tinge in winter (no white tip to tail at any time); b) 'blue fox' with uniform

199

Arctic fox *Alopex lagopus* (summer coat).

Arctic fox *Alopex lagopus* (winter coat).

200

smoky grey coat throughout year ('blues' form 1–5% of population but in some areas (eg Iceland) over 50%). Head and body 50–65cm (20–26in), tail 28–33cm (11–13in), height at shoulder 30cm (12in), weight 4·5–8kg (10–18lb).

Range: throughout Arctic, including islands, also mountain chain of Scandinavia, move southwards in summer.

Habitat: tundra.

Life history: breeds April, gestation 6 weeks, may have two litters a year, second in July–August, of 5–8 young.

Feeding: main prey voles and lemmings, ground-nesting birds, carrion, shellfish. Also some plants. Stores food in crevices in rocks.

Habits: Extremely tame, enters camps and takes food from hand.

Populations: numbers rise and fall with those of voles and lemmings. Statistics from fur trade show a four-yearly cycle of abundance.

POLAR BEAR

ORDER	Carnivora
FAMILY	Ursidae
GENUS	*Thalarctos*
SPECIES	*T. maritimus*

Description: most carnivorous and one of largest of bears, distinguished

Polar bear *Thalarctos maritimus*.

from other bears by 'Roman' nose, small ears and eyes, long neck, large feet with hairy soles, larger canines and smaller molars. Coat white with

a tinge of cream or yellow. Male head and body 200–280cm (7–9ft), tail 8–10cm (3–4in), height at shoulder up to 155cm (5ft), weight up to 640kg (1600lb). Female smaller, averages 280kg (700lb) weight.

Range and habitat: Arctic seas, on coasts in some areas, seldom ventures far inland.

Life history: mates in July, gestation 240 days, cubs 1–4, usually 1, born February while mother in den in snow in state of winter dormancy (not hibernation). At birth 31 cm (12in) long, weight 0·6kg (1½lb), with coat of short sparse hair. Ears open 26 days, eyes open 33 days, starts to walk at 47 days, weaned April but remains with mother until 10 months old. Sexually mature 2½–4 years. Longevity 33 years.

Feeding: seals favourite prey, stalked while hauled out, also whale and seal carrion, and fish.

Habits: solitary, ambles over ice using hairy soles, occasionally gallops, never trots, swings head from side-to-side, searching for prey. Expert but slow swimmer, dives well, can remain submerged for two minutes. Usually male does not den up for winter.

Food of the Polar bear: (1) seals, (2) lemmings, (3) carrion such as whales, (4) fish, (5) eggs and (6) birds.

REINDEER

ORDER	Artiodactyla
FAMILY	Cervidae
GENUS	*Rangifer*
SPECIES	*R. tarandus*

Description: differs from all other deer (except Caribou) in females having antlers. Coat thick, muzzle hairy, ears small, tail very short, hoofs broad, flat, deeply cleft so that they splay giving support on snow.

202

Reindeer *Rangifer tarandus.*

Male head and body 185–215cm (6½ft), height at shoulder 105–120cm (3½ft), weight 120–150kg (48–60lb), females weigh 110kg (275lb).

Range: southern Norway, northern Finland and Russia. Introduced herd in Cairngorms of Scotland.

Habitat: tundra and taiga.

Life history: breeds September–October. Gestation 230–246 days, 1–2 calves at birth, young walk in a few hours, weaned at 2 months.

Feeding: summer: grasses, sedges, herbaceous plants, lemmings, birds' eggs. Winter: lichens (reindeer moss, species of the *Cladonia*), buds and shoots of shrubs.

Habits: females and young live in herds, males in separate herds, old males solitary. Mature males join herds at rut and form harems, each mature male holding a harem. After rut males leave herds but follow them during winter, shedding antlers then and re-growing them in following April. Females shed antlers May–June. Rutting call is a loud grunt repeated three times.

Footprint of Reindeer.

ERRATICS

The word 'erratics' has been used advisedly, much in the sense in which it is used in geology, for objects found where they do not properly belong. In this instance it is living objects, whereas in geology the word is applied to rocks or stones. To some degree the House mouse, Brown rat and Black rat should be added to the list of species included under this heading. All three originated in central Asia and all three have made their way across Europe partly unaided, partly by human agency, the House mouse probably in prehistoric times, the Black rat at about the 12th century and the Brown rat in the 16th–17th centuries. To treat these as non-indigenous would, however, pose an unanswerable question about what constitutes an indigenous species, for if we go far enough back in time most mammalian species are intruders or partial intruders into Europe from elsewhere, especially since the close of the Ice Age.

A few of those species treated here as erratics clearly merit the title. The Hoary bat, a North American species, that turned up in the Orkneys, clearly does not belong there. Similarly, the Egyptian slit-faced bat, found on Corfu, is an African species and the Ikonnikov's bat, although recorded from Sofia and the Ruthenian Carpathians, can only be a straggler from Asia, where the species is widespread. All these can fly, so the occurrence of occasional vagrants is not surprising. Even a terrestrial species like Ognev's dormouse, which is found in Bulgaria near the Turkish frontier, is an Asiatic species and may have arrived there accidentally in cargo or baggage. The same is probably true of the Cairo spiny mouse, an African species confined to Crete.

The presence of the Barbary ape on Gibraltar has long presented a puzzle. What can be taken as certain is that if it were not cared for, it would soon disappear from that locality. Presumably, therefore, it can be no more than a local introduction. The Genet, Porcupine and Egyptian mongoose have been long established and are fairly widely distributed in southern Europe, where they were formerly thought to have arrived by natural means. Opinion is now veering to the idea that they were originally brought over from Africa by man.

The remaining erratics are, with

the exception of the Musk-ox and the Saiga, either introduced into Europe to be ranched for their fur, brought in as park deer or introduced as pets. All are introductions of fairly recent date, that is, within the last hundred years, seldom more. The first group includes the Muskrat, Coypu, Raccoon dog and American mink. The second includes the four species of deer. The third includes the Grey squirrel and the Raccoon. Escapers from fur ranches are not infrequent and since the ranches themselves tend to be numerous and widely distributed, the chances of pairs forming among those that go feral, and of the species becoming established in the wild, are high.

This does not mean that there will necessarily be a steady build up of populations and an extension of their range. The Edible dormouse, indigenous to continental Europe, was introduced into England in 1902 and has become thoroughly established, but it has remained confined to an area of about 155sq km (60sq mi). The American mink, by contrast, which went feral much later, has spread widely, using the waterways. The Muskrat, also aqua-tic or semi-aquatic, has taken advantage of the same means of dispersal and its spread has been spectacular, although this may be more correctly attributed to its having been deliberately released in many widely separated parts of Europe.

The Coypu has fluctuated in numbers and distribution because it is susceptible to cold winters. Other introduced species have also fluctuated although the causes may not be known for certain. The Musk-ox, for example, was introduced or re-introduced into Iceland, Spitzbergen, Norway and Sweden. It dies out from time to time in Iceland and Sweden. The Saiga, the other of the two exceptions mentioned earlier, has been re-introduced onto the steppes of southwestern Russia, from which it was formerly wiped out, and has now established itself in large numbers.

The spread of the Grey squirrel in Britain since the 1890s has also been spectacular. One observation that may be instructive in this respect concerns a pair known to have migrated 17.5km (11mi) before settling down, although they passed through suitable country on the way.

EGYPTIAN SLIT-FACED OR HOLLOW-FACED BAT

ORDER	Chiroptera
FAMILY	Nycteridae
GENUS	*Nycteris*
SPECIES	*N. thebaica*

Description: head and body 47–75mm (2–3in), tail similar length, forearm 50mm (2in), weight 21g ($\frac{3}{4}$oz). Ears large. Distinguish-able from all other European bats by the possession of a groove in face that ends in a pit on forehead. Island of Corfu.

IKONNIKOV'S BAT

ORDER	Chiroptera
FAMILY	Vespertilionidae
GENUS	*Myotis*
SPECIES	*M. ikonnikovi*

Description: very like Whiskered bat (p. 106) but smaller head and body 37–42mm (1$\frac{1}{2}$in), forearm 30–33mm (1in). Sofia and Ruthenian Carpathians.

Ikonnikov's bat *Myotis ikonnikovi*.

BRANDT'S BAT

ORDER	Chiroptera
FAMILY	Vespertilionidae
GENUS	*Myotis*
SPECIES	*M. brandtii*

Description: slightly larger than Whiskered bat. It was not until 1958 that certain individual bats, looking like Whiskered bats, were closely examined and accepted as a sub-species of *Myotis mystacinus*. This was elevated to specific rank in 1970 and named *M. brandtii*. Apart from size, the main differences are in the characters of the skull. The most readily observable are the shape and size of the two premolars. (Fossil remains of this new species have been found in the Pleistocene, in Hungary, suggesting that the species reached Europe before the Whiskered bat.)

In addition to being found from Poland and Hungary to France and the Low Countries, *M. brandtii* has recently been identified in the British Isles.

HOARY BAT

ORDER	Chiroptera
FAMILY	Vespertilionidae
GENUS	*Lasiurus*
SPECIES	*L. cinereus*

Description: head and body 100mm (4in), tail 37mm (1½in), forearm 52mm (2in), wingspan 400mm (16in), weight 42g (1½oz). Ears short, rounded, with naked black margins. Leaves roost after nightfall and second flight two hours before sunrise. Flies high and swiftly. One specimen found in Orkneys, another in Iceland.

Hoary bat *Lasiurus cinereus*.

BARBARY APE

ORDER	Primates
FAMILY	Cercopithecidae
GENUS	*Macaca*
SPECIES	*M. sylvanus*

Description: almost tailless monkey with black and yellow fur giving a mottled yellow-grey effect. Limbs of equal length. Forehead and crown covered with erect golden-brown hairs. Face relatively short, dark flesh-colour. Brow ridges meet over nose. Head and body 60cm (2ft), weight up to 11kg (24lb).

Range: Morocco, Gibraltar (introduced?), believed to have been originally a native of south-east Asia.

Habitat: rocky country.

Food of the Barbary ape: (1) insects, (2) twigs and (3) fruits.

Life history: no set breeding season. Births occur throughout year. Gestation 210 days. Babies almost hairless at birth nursed by mother for a year.

Feeding: food includes leaves, pine cones and fruit, insects, scorpions and a variety of small invertebrates. May be pests to crops or from descending on a town in search of food.

Habits: diurnal, spends night in holes or crevices in rock. Good climber. Said to post sentries. Has good eye-sight.

Barbary ape *Macaca sylvanus*.

Special features: legend that if Barbary apes leave Gibraltar British will lose it. Result: Barbary apes on Gibraltar given care and protection with a junior officer of Artillery in charge of their welfare.

GREY SQUIRREL

ORDER	Rodentia
FAMILY	Sciuridae
GENUS	*Sciurus*
SPECIES	*S. carolinensis*

Description: speckled grey above and white on underparts in winter with only slight brownish ear-tufts, white hairs behind ears. Tail fairly bushy fringed with white in winter. In summer coat shorter and more brownish with a bright rufous streak along flanks and on paws. Body hair moulted April and September, moult lasting 5 to 6 weeks. Hairs of tail and ears replaced once a year. Albinos occasionally, also melanics. Erythristic forms occur sporadically. Some young more reddish-brown than adults. Adult: average head and body length 259mm (10·3in), maximum 280mm (11·1in). Tail 215mm (8·5in) average, maximum 240mm (9·5in). Weight 510–570g (18–20oz), varies with food abundance.

Range: native of eastern North America, introduced British Isles 19th century. Spread rapidly. Now in most English and Welsh counties and some Irish and Scottish counties.

Habitat: open woodlands and parklands, typically mixed woodland with mature trees, especially oak. Lower altitudes than Red squirrel.

Life history: pre-mating period often marked by males chasing female until dominant male drives others away. Breeding season, end of December to June. Gestation 44 days. Generally 2 litters a year of 1 to 7 young (average 3). Naked and blind at birth weighing 13 to 17g (c. 5oz). Weaned at 7–10 weeks, young reach adult size at 8 months and are sexually mature at 6–11 months.

Feeding: food sought at all levels in woodland, in hedgerows and open fields. Mainly vegetarian but some small animal food taken. Feeding sometimes communal but social

Grey squirrel *Sciurus caroliensis*.

Grey squirrel in summer coat.

dominance observed. On rare occasions make hoards in cavities in trees. Normally nuts, acorns and other food buried singly and well spread out. Buried food found by smell, even when ground snow-covered. May not necessarily return to food it has itself buried. Often food carried some distance (up to 180m (200yd)) to be buried. Leaf-cutting, bark-stripping, eating green buds of young trees makes squirrels unpopular with foresters. Paws used to open biscuit tins. Pillage bird-tables. Acorns most important food, then nuts, beech mast, toadstools and other fungi, seeds of many trees, bulbs, roots, shoots, buds, catkins, sappy bark, insects, occasionally eggs and flesh (House sparrows) eaten, carrion possibly. Oak galls torn open to eat insect larvae. Bones and lead garden labels chewed.

Habits: two kinds of nest made. Winter drey, also used for nursery, made of leafy twigs, domed and usually in angle between branch and trunk. Lined with leaves, bark, moss or grass and especially honeysuckle bark. Summer drey is a leafy platform built out on branches. Sleeps in drey at night. Groups of males, non-breeding females and juveniles may share nests. Territorial instinct strong in females with young who may drive other squirrels from nest-tree. Diurnal; activity peaks early morning and before dusk with minor peak at midday. No hibernation, possibly less active in very cold weather. Occasionally taken by Stoats, dogs; rarely by foxes, hawks, owls. Sound made by males chasing females low and vibrating like song of grasshopper. Bark, response to danger, very rapid. As danger recedes slows down to scolding, chuk-chuk-chuk-quaa. Purrs when feeding. Also chattering and scolding.

Population: regarded in British Isles as pest but attempts to exterminate it have failed largely due to squirrel's ability to keep out of sight among trees. Fall in numbers associated with beech mast failure and severe winters.

Special features: can travel on ground at 29kmph (18mph) in bounds of 1–1·5m (3–5ft). Can leap 3·6m (12ft) from tree to tree. Standing jump of 3m (10ft). Swims well using hind feet only; 8km (5 miles) across lake. Can climb vertical, rough-cast walls and travel along horizontal wires. Sight main sense, long-sighted, no need to move eyes, can see all round. Can detect slightest movement because retina made up of cones only. Good sense of smell, hearing good.

MOUSE-LIKE OR OGNEV'S DORMOUSE

ORDER	Rodentia
FAMILY	Gliridae
GENUS	*Myomimus*
SPECIES	*M. personatus*

Description: mouse-like, upperparts yellowish-grey with white underparts and a sharp line of demarcation between, tail thinly-haired with short white hairs. Head and body 61–110mm (2½–4in) long, tail 59–78mm (2⅓–3in) long.

First described in 1924 from a specimen from Turkmenistan near the frontier with Iran, more recently found again in south-eastern Bulgaria. Virtually nothing known about its biology. Believed to be terrestrial, possibly burrowing.

MUSKRAT

ORDER	Rodentia
FAMILY	Microtidae
GENUS	*Ondatra*
SPECIES	*O. zibethicus*

Description: large thickset vole, intermediate in size between water vole and coypu, dark brown with underparts dirty-white. Eyes and ears small. Head and body 260–400mm (10–16in), tail, laterally compressed, 190–275mm (7½–11in), weight 600–1700g (1lb 5½oz–3lb 12oz).

Range: native of North America, now feral in much of central and northern Europe from France, Belgium and Holland to Finland, Poland, Czechoslovakia and Hungary.

Habitat: slow-flowing rivers and lakes.

Lodge of Muskrat.

Life history: gestation 21–23

Muskrat *Ondatra zibethicus.*

days. Several litters a year of 4–8 young, weaned at 30 days.

Feeding: riverside plants and also green and root crops. Some animal food, such as freshwater mussels.

Habits: active mainly at night, also by day. Swims fast using hindlegs and tail, dives and swims far under-

water to escape detection. Burrows into banks but also builds lodges of twigs, reeds, rushes, grass, in shallow water. Musk glands used to mark territory. Voice a sharp whistle.

Special features: introduced as a ranched animal for fur, then escaped or deliberately released. Great damage to river banks and crops.

CAIRO SPINY MOUSE

ORDER	Rodentia
FAMILY	Muridae
GENUS	*Acomys*
SPECIES	*A. cahirinus*

Description: pale reddish-brown above, white underparts, large ears, long tail, back coated with conspicuous flattened bristles ('spines').

Head and body 95–130mm (4–5in) long, tail slightly longer.

Range: Cyprus, Crete (both

probably introduced), Asia (Israel to Pakistan) most of Africa.

Habitat: rocky, dry areas, enters houses in winter (susceptible to lowered temperatures).

Life history: gestation 42 days, litters 1–5, eyes open at birth, weaned at 2 weeks.

Feeding: plant food, especially grain, but also omnivorous.

Habits: lives in rock crevices. Good climber.

Cairo spiny mouse *Acomys cahirinus*.

CRESTED PORCUPINE

ORDER	Rodentia
FAMILY	Hystricidae
GENUS	*Hystrix*
SPECIES	*H. cristata*

Description: stout-bodied, moderately short-legged, brownish-black with white band under neck

Crested porcupine *Hystrix cristata*.

and halfway up sides. Head and neck with crest of long bristles, brown below, white above. Body quills of two kinds, long and slender, short and stout, banded black and white. Quills on rump black, on tail white. Head and body up to 70cm (28in) long, tail 5—12cm (2—5in), weight 10—15kg (25—38lb).

Range: Italy, Sicily, Albania, Yugoslavia (probably all introductions), northern half of Africa (Morocco to Egypt, Sudan, south to Senegal and East Africa).

Habitat: rocky hills with vegetation cover.

Life history: mates in spring, gestation 63—112 days, 2—4 young born late spring or early summer in nest of leaves, grass and roots. Eyes open at birth, quills soft, harden in 10 days.

Feeding: mainly roots, also herbaceous plants, bark; menace to root crops.

Habits: mainly nocturnal, solitary or in pairs, rests in natural holes in ground or among rocks. Erects quills in defence, rattles quills and vibrates tail as warning, then rushes backwards at enemy. Quills easily detached, become embedded in foe. Voice a muffled growl.

COYPU OR NUTRIA

ORDER	Rodentia
FAMILY	Capromyidae
GENUS	*Myocastor*
SPECIES	*M. coypus*

Description: one of largest rodents. Stout body, massive head, large, orange-yellow incisors, short, round hairy ears with tuft of black hair in centre, squarish muzzle and thick, bristly, scaly tail. Front legs short with strong claws, hind legs longer with webbed feet. Dark brown, blackish or gingery fur on back; thick, soft, water-repellent, grey fur on underparts ('nutria' of commerce). Total length half is tail. Weight 6—9kg (12—20lb).

Range: South American species. Kept in captivity for fur in North America, Europe and temperate Asia; escapers have established feral populations.

Habitat: river banks, reed-beds and marshes.

Life history: breeds throughout year. Gestation 100—132 days. Usually 2 litters a year of 2—9 (usually 5—6) young. Furred with eyes open at birth, move around in few

Coypu or Nutria *Myocastor coypus*.

hours. Suckled in water; female's teats high up on flanks. Weaned at 7–8 weeks. Sexually mature at 3 months.

Feeding: water and marsh plants, especially reeds and sedges. Occasionally mussels. In Britain when numbers increased agricultural crops attacked, especially sugar beet and kale; grass and green cereals grazed.

Habits: solitary; crepuscular and nocturnal; active by day if frosty. Makes runs through vegetation. Burrows in river banks for short refuges. Breeding nests of reeds and marsh plants piled above ground level. Moves slowly on land but powerful swimmer. Can inflict fierce bites on dogs or trappers but normally docile. Voice: low grunts, humming noise when swimming, hisses when disturbed, harsh scream when distressed. Also grinds teeth and clicks incisors violently when captured. Young preyed on by Weasel, Otter, Brown rat, owls and hawks.

Special features: farming of Coypus in Britain for their fur started in 1930's and when animals escaped they helped to clear watercourses by eating vegetation. When numbers increased habits changed and banks of rivers damaged with burrows and crops destroyed. In 1962 extermination campaign carried out and Coypu now restricted to inaccessible Broads of East Anglia.

RACCOON DOG

ORDER	Carnivora
FAMILY	Canidae
GENUS	*Nyctereutes*
SPECIES	*N. procyonoides*

Description: fox-like but heavy build, short-legged, bushy tail, dark brown fur but ash-grey on head and neck with dark patches around eyes (as in raccoon). Tuft of long hair behind each eye. Total length 75cm (2½ft) of which 15–18cm (6–7in) is tail.

Range: eastern Asia, introduced to European Russia for fur, has spread to Finland, Sweden, Poland, East Germany.

Habitat: river valleys, grassy and willow-studded plains. Also coniferous forests in Europe.

Life history: mates April, gestation in two months, litter of 6–8 born June, in burrow.

Feeding: omnivorous with partiality for fish, plant food in autumn such as pulp fruits and acorns.

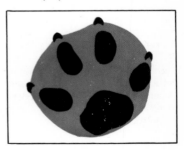

Footprint of Raccoon dog.

215

Habits: fox-like but hibernates (incompletely), lives solitary or in family parties, male remaining until young independent.

Raccoon dog *Nyctereutes procyonoides.*

RACCOON

ORDER	Carnivora
FAMILY	Procyonidae
GENUS	*Procyon*
SPECIES	*P. lotor*

Description: stout-bodied, short-legged with bushy tail. Fur greyish-brown, tail ringed with white. White markings on face and conspicuous dark band across eyes ('highwayman's mask'). Total length 75cm (2½ft), including tail 25cm (10in), weight up to 10kg (25lb).

Range: North America to northern South America. Introduced West Germany and Byelorussia, spread to Luxembourg, Netherlands.

Habitat: wooded country near streams.

Life history: mating January to June (according to whether it hibernates or not). Gestation 63–70 days. Litters of 3–6 young, eyes open at 19 days, remain with parents for rest of year.

Feeding: mainly aquatic animals, especially crayfish, but include insects, molluscs, fish, frogs, freshwater turtles. Also, some plant food.

Habits: agile, skilful climber, nocturnal, seldom swims. Toes on forefeet as deft as fingers (idea that raccoon always washes food is an exaggeration although some food is dunked: no ready explanation for this). Hibernation in northern parts of range.

Raccoon *Procyon lotor*.

Raccoon dunking its food before eating.

Food of the Raccoon: (1) insects, (2) fish, (3) small mammals, (4) plants and sometimes (5) birds.

AMERICAN MINK

ORDER	Carnivora
FAMILY	Mustelidae
GENUS	*Mustela*
SPECIES	*M. vison*

Description: long, slender body slung low, ears short, set close together, bushy tail, short legs, toes partly webbed. Thick fur uniformly rich dark brown, small white spot on lower lip and chin and sometimes few white hairs or scattered white spots on underside. Numerous colour mutations produced under domestication from white to almost black. Head and body length 302–430mm (12–17in), tail 127–229mm (5–9in), weight 565–1020g ($1\frac{1}{4}$–$2\frac{1}{4}$lb).

Range: native of most of Canada and USA. Kept on fur farms in many parts of the world including Europe where escapers have built up feral populations. Deliberately introduced into Russia where it has spread widely.

Habitat: by streams, rivers and lakes.

Life history: breeding February to early April. Delayed implantation. Gestation 45–50 days but may be 39–76 days. 5–6 kits in litter but up to 17 recorded.

Feeding: Water voles, frogs, newts, trout, crayfish and molluscs. Has become menace by killing poultry, pheasants, waterfowl and domestic rabbits. In Scandinavia feral mink endangering salmon stocks and in Iceland prey on wild birds, especially ground-nesters such as waders.

Habits: nocturnal and solitary. Dens in clefts of rocks or enlarged Water vole holes. Swims well and catches much food in water. Males range over long distances, females stay within small home range. Usually silent but both sexes purr during mating season. Shrieks when alarmed.

Special features: one of most valuable fur bearers, has been bred commercially since 1866 on large

American mink *Mustela vison*.

farms and ranches in North America and Europe. In 1951 pelts of 2 million ranch-reared mink sold on United States market.

EGYPTIAN MONGOOSE OR ICHNEUMON

ORDER	Carnivora
FAMILY	Viverridae
GENUS	*Herpestes*
SPECIES	*H. ichneumon*

Description: long body, fur grizzled iron-grey, short legs, long, black-tipped tail tapering from a broad base, short broad ears, claws non-retractile. Head and body 60cm (24in), tail 45cm (18in), weight 8kg (20lb).

Range: southern third of Iberian peninsula. Africa (Egypt to the Cape).

Habitat: scrub to woodlands, lowlands to high plateaux.

Life history: mating in April, gestation up to 104 days, births in July–August, 2–4 in a litter.

Feeding: probably rodents, reptiles, insects, occasionally birds.

Egyptian mongoose or Ichneumon *Herpestes ichneumon.*

Habits: solitary or in pairs, occasionally in groups up to 14. Hunts day or night, mainly nocturnal but has colour vision. Digs own burrow. Mainly silent, occasional whistle. (Sacred to Egyptians).

EUROPEAN, FELINE OR SMALL-SPOTTED GENET

ORDER	Carnivora
FAMILY	Viverridae
GENUS	*Genetta*
SPECIES	*G. genetta*

Description: cat-like but more slender, elegant build. Fur soft, spot-

European, Feline or Small-spotted genet *Genetta genetta*.

ted or blotched with black on a light ground. Tail ringed with dark and light bands. Crest of erectile hairs along back. Head and body 55cm (22in) long, tail 45cm (18in) long, weight up to 2·2kg (4·8lb). Face tapering to pointed muzzle. Ears prominent, oval, eyes moderately large, whiskers long. Legs short, toes with retractile claws, 5 toes on forefeet, 4 on hindfeet.

Range: Iberian Peninsula, including Balearics, southern and western France. Most of sub-Saharan Africa.

Habitat: bush country.

Chinese water deer *Hydropotes inermis.*

Life history: gestation 70–77 days. Two litters a year, in April and August–September, of 1–3 young, eyes open at 8 days, weaned at 25 days. Longevity up to 21 years.

Feeding: small birds and mammals, insects, some grass. Stalks prey moving snake-like through grass with tail extended, body lowered. Seizes prey with front paws and teeth, rolls over on side and seizes also with hindfeet to hold moderate-sized prey (eg rat).

Habits: nocturnal, mainly solitary, terrestrial but readily climbs bushes and trees. In aggressive display erects dorsal crest, fluffs hair of tail to form 'bottle brush', purrs loudly.

CHINESE WATER DEER

ORDER	Artiodactyla
FAMILY	Cervidae
GENUS	*Hydropotes*
SPECIES	*H. inermis*

Description: small deer unique amongst Cervidae in completely lacking antlers and in possessing inguinal scent glands. Male has long curved movable canines, smaller in female. Coat pale brown stippled with black with white around nose and eyes, inside ears and on chin. Pointed, narrow ears. Small dark tail. Height at shoulder 50cm (20in), head and body length 90cm (35in), tail 6cm (2in), weight up to 16kg (35lb).

Range: native of China from Yangtze Kiang north to Korea. Escaped from captivity in southern England and France and formed feral populations.

Habitat: in native China inhabits swamp country but in Britain adapted to dry woodland and open country.

Life history: rut in December, fawns born late May to early June. In China 5–6 fawns but fewer in Europe. Fawns sparsely and indistinctly spotted in lines.

Feeding: more of a grazer than other small deer in Europe; mainly grasses, but also vegetables and root crops.

Habits: solitary and diurnal. Bounding run 'like a rabbit'. Whistling call by males during rut; alarm call a scream like that of a wounded hare.

CHINESE OR REEVE'S MUNTJAC

ORDER	Artiodactyla
FAMILY	Cervidae
GENUS	*Muntiacus*
SPECIES	*M. reevesi*

Description: small primitive deer with dark reddish coat, white chin, throat and rump. Male has short simple antlers with single brow tine mounted on long hairy pedicles; long tusk-like upper canines. Female's coat lighter in colour and black tufts of hair replace antlers. Face marked longitudinally by two slit-like openings of facial scent glands, hence alternative name of rib-faced deer. Fairly long tail with bushy tip. Higher at rump than shoulder. Height at shoulder 37·5–42·5cm (15–17in), antlers 10cm (4n), weight 18–22kg (40–50lb), female weight 13kg (30lb).

Range: native of southern China, introduced into parks in southern and central England and parts of France. Escapers have formed feral populations.

Habitat: originally in subtropical forest; feral populations live in woodland with dense, scrubby undergrowth but graze in clearings.

Life-history: bucks and does associate October to March. One, sometimes two, fawns born in late summer, but have been recorded in November and December. Fawns dark brown, white spotted on flanks.

Feeding: browsing and grazing on shrubs, grass, roots and fruits. Damage to farm crops and orchards and some bark-stripping.

Habits: diurnal and crepuscular but not often seen because concealed in dense undergrowth. Usually solitary

Chinese or Reeve's muntjac *Muntiacus reevesi.*

or in pairs. Trees frayed by males during rut and marked with scent from frontal and sub-orbital glands. Call a short, dog-like bark produced by expulsion of breath, hence alternative name of barking deer. Fawns vulnerable to predation by foxes.

Both Indian muntjac (*M. muntjak*) and Chinese muntjac originally kept in parks in England but Indian species no longer present although it may have interbred with *M. reevesi.*

SIKA DEER

ORDER	Artiodactyla
FAMILY	Cervidae
GENUS	*Cervus*
SPECIES	*C. nippon*

Description: closely related to Red deer with antlers similar but simpler, with never more than four points. In summer, flanks warm buff-brown with faint spots, deep brown in winter. Head paler and greyer than

flanks. Short pure white tail. When flushed, rump shows as white heart-shaped patch with black borders. Slight mane. Antlers cast in early April, in velvet May to July, cleaned by September. Male height at shoul-

der 82–90cm (32–35in), nose to tail c. 150cm (60in), weight c. 63kg (140lb). Female smaller.

Range: small isolated localities in eastern Asia from Vladivostok to southern China, on all main islands of Japan and on Formosa. Introduced into parks in Europe. Escapers have formed feral populations in Britain, Ireland, Denmark, Germany, France and Austria.

Habitat: broadleaved woodlands in Asia. In Europe open woodland,

Sika deer *Cervus nippon*.

heath and moor, sometimes wet ground such as estuarine reed-beds.

Life history: rut starts end of September, peak in October, ends by November. Male polygamous herding 5–6 hinds. Usually only one calf born late May or June, similar to that of fallow deer but with smaller spots. Interbreeds with Red deer.

Rump, antler and footprint of Sika deer.

Feeding: mainly grass and rough herbage, but will also strip bark, especially hazel, and browse young shoots. Occasionally feed on field crops.

Habits: moves with heavy pounding gallop, similar to Red deer. Except during rut stags solitary or in small groups, especially at end of winter. Hinds and young in separate groups during winter. Nocturnal; spends day in thick cover. During rut, stags have penetrating whistle rising and falling and ending in grunt. Sharp scream of alarm.

WHITE-TAILED OR VIRGINIAN DEER

ORDER	Artiodactyla
FAMILY	Cervidae
GENUS	*Odocoileus*
SPECIES	*O. virginianus*

Description: medium-sized with fairly short branching antlers, curving forwards. Coat reddish-brown in summer, greyish brown in winter, prominent white tail patch displayed in flight. Height at shoulder 106cm (3½ft), weight up to 136kg (300lb).

White-tailed or Virginian deer *Odocoileus virginianus*.

Range: United States (east of Great Plains). Introduced (1934) and now feral in south-western Finland.

Habitat: forests with little bushy undergrowth.

Life history: rut takes place in November, one buck serving 2–3 does. Gestation 210–250 days. Usually twins, occasionally 3 fawns at a birth, each 1·3–2·4kg (3–5lb), suckled every 4 hours, follow dam at 4–6 weeks. Weaned and lose spots at 4 months.

Feeding: mainly leaves, including conifer foliage, but also herbaceous plants and grass.

Habits: small parties of females and young unite in winter forming a 'yard'.

MUSK-OX

ORDER	Artiodactyla
FAMILY	Bovidae
GENUS	*Ovibos*
SPECIES	*O. moschatus*

Description: cattle-like but related to goat-antelopes. Dense coat of deep brown, shaggy hair, reaching almost to ground in winter. Horns like meat-hooks, meeting in centre of head. Muzzle hairy, hoofs broad, males with musk-gland on face. Head and body 220cm (6½ft), tail 10cm (4in), height at shoulder 150cm (5ft), weight up to 400kg (880lb). Females smaller than males.

Range: North American Arctic. Introduced in Spitzbergen and southern Norway.

Habitat: tundra.

Musk-ox *Ovibos moschatus.*

Life history: single calf at birth, born May, 45cm (18in) at shoulder, follows cow at 1 hour.

Feeding: sparse vegetation.

Habits: forms phalanx for protection against Wolves of calves or injured comrade.

Special features: habit of forming a phalanx effective against Wolves. Against man armed with gun it has been disastrous, since pelt valued as sleigh rug and hunter must kill one after another of herd to obtain one pelt.

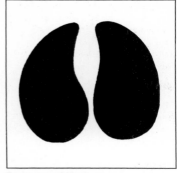

Footprint of Musk-ox.

Phalanx of Musk-ox formed for protection against wolves.

SAIGA

ORDER	Artiodactyla
FAMILY	Bovidae
GENUS	*Saiga*
SPECIES	*S. tatarica*

Description: antelope noted for its puffy nose which probably warms the air it breathes. Characteristics of sheep-goat group and gazelle group: long incisor teeth like sheep but some skull characters and glands on front legs, feet, face and in groin like those of gazelles. Muzzle enlarged and puffy with nostrils overhanging mouth like short proboscis. Horns, in male only, slightly lyre-shaped, strongly ringed, amber-

Saiga *Saiga tatarica*.

coloured, about 30cm (1ft) long. Short, woolly, buff coat in summer, thicker, longer and almost white in winter. Height at shoulder 75–80cm (30–32in), weight 40–50kg (80–100lb).

Range: southeast Russia and parts of central Asia.

Habitat: open steppe country from sea level to 1600m (5000ft).

Life history: rut in December, rams fight for harems of up to 50 ewes. Mass-mating period of about a week. Gestation 4 months, 1–3 young, usually twins, born in April, lie in cover for first few days, then join mother. High mortality in lambs, 10% eaten by Wolves, foxes or eagles, or lost by mother. Mother will defend young, jumping into air and lashing out with hoofs. Further 10% killed by predation or starvation within a month, and cold snowy winter kills more. By following April only 40% remain. Females sexually mature 8 months, males 20 months. Many males so exhausted by rutting fights they fall easy prey to Wolves.

Feeding: grass and low-growing cespitose and wormwood.

Habits: rests during hottest part of day in summer, active at dusk, active also in day in winter. Live in large herds of both males and females, disperse into separate male and female herds in early spring, migrating northwards in search of new pastures. In April males solitary or in small groups while ewes give birth. In August and September migrate south, re-forming into large herds until they break up for rut. During migrations herds move at 5–19kmph (3–12mph). Sudden panics set whole herd massing together and running for miles at 80kmph (50mph), heads held low off ground, probably mobile nostrils keep out dust. While running individuals take occasional leaps.

Special features: overhunting and a succession of droughts reduced numbers in Russia and Asia to about 1000 in 1930. Slowly, under strict protection, they increased to a population explosion, especially in Asia. In European Russia numbers reached half a million by 1958. Today they are maintained and cropped for their meat which is said to be extremely good.

MARINE

The marine environment poses a number of problems for mammals that can be appreciated only if one understands how mammals have evolved since their origins 30 million years ago. From the beginning mammals evolved on dry land and many of their characteristics are adaptations to a terrestial environment. They have lungs because they breathe air; their limbs are variously modified for running or climbing; and, because air is not a dense medium and offers very little resistance to moving objects, their bodies are not streamlined.

To live successfully in an aquatic environment an animal needs to overcome the fact that there is far less oxygen in water than in air and that water is a dense medium. As a result the only mammals to have colonized marine environments are those which have evolved methods of obtaining air in spite of being submerged for sometimes considerable periods; which have limbs modified to form paddles or organs more appropriate to locomotion in water; and which have streamlined bodies that overcome water resistance. Not surprisingly, only a few groups have undergone the extreme modifications required to solve these problems and, as a result, marine mammals are members of but three orders; the Cetacea (whales, dol-

phins and porpoises); the Pinnipedia (seals, sealions and walruses); and the Sirenia (the Sea cows). The pinnipeds are less adapted to a wholly aquatic life than are the cetaceans, and can make use of the land to a limited extent for resting, basking and, in the majority of species, breeding. The most important adaptations are the conversion of limbs to flippers, the development of a layer of blubber under the skin giving insulation from a cold medium yet allowing the escape of body heat when necessary, and a fundamental reorganisation of the respiratory and blood-vascular systems enabling these mammals to dive, remain submerged for long periods, and even to sleep below the surface, rising automatically and periodically to the surface to breathe.

Cetaceans, on the other hand, show extreme adaptations to their aquatic environment. Their bodies are streamlined and resemble the torpedo shape more usually associated with fish. Their tails are extraordinarily fish-like but are different in that they flap in the vertical plane rather than the horizontal. Associated with the streamlined bodyform is a reduction of the length of the neck.

Feeding relationships. Although a completely different medium, the

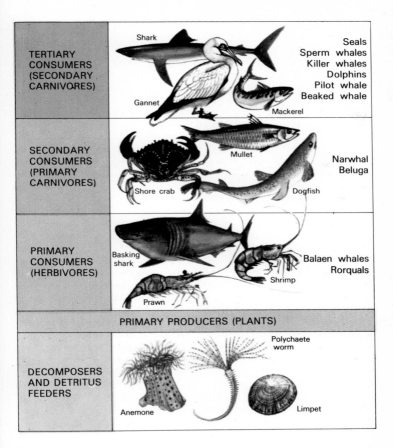

TERTIARY CONSUMERS (SECONDARY CARNIVORES)	Shark, Gannet, Mackerel	Seals Sperm whales Killer whales Dolphins Pilot whale Beaked whale
SECONDARY CONSUMERS (PRIMARY CARNIVORES)	Shore crab, Mullet, Dogfish	Narwhal Beluga
PRIMARY CONSUMERS (HERBIVORES)	Basking shark, Shrimp, Prawn	Balaen whales Rorquals
PRIMARY PRODUCERS (PLANTS)		
DECOMPOSERS AND DETRITUS FEEDERS	Anemone, Polychaete worm, Limpet	

trophic structure of the marine environment runs on the same principles as for land. The decomposer and detritus-feeder level consists of a bewildering profusion of minute crustacea and larvae of other animal groups which can be classed together as the zooplankton. These feed on microscopic plants and dead organic matter. Their nutrient wealth is such that they form the basic diet of the large balaen whales and the Basking shark, not to mention the vast schools of smaller fish that support man's fisheries. Important also are the polychaetes and sea anemones, jelly-fish and comb-jellies.

The primary carnivores are mainly fish such as Herring and Cod though some sharks also take filter feeders. Nearly all the marine animals feed at one time or another on the invertebrates but in the Narwhal and Beluga these are the staple diet. Carnivorous invertebrates include the Seamouse and the crabs.

The order Pinnipedia or flapfooted animals consists of three families: the Phocidae or true seals, sometimes called the earless seals, the Otariidae or eared seals and the Odobenidae containing the Walrus. Eared seals are not found in North Atlantic waters but there are seven species of true seals that breed in European waters including Iceland and the Walrus is an occasional visitor to the waters of north-western Europe.

All pinnipedes are well adapted for marine life in their anatomy, physiology and behaviour, but all come onto ice floes or on land to breed. The body is streamlined and padded with blubber for insulation. All four limbs are reduced to webbed flippers.

The true seals are distinguished by having no visible external ear (it is hidden within the earhole and is very small) and an inability to tuck the hindflippers under the body for walking. The eared seals have a small external ear flap and can bring the hindflippers forward for walking on land, as in sealions. True seals swim by sideways flapping of the hindflippers, the foreflippers being used for manoeuvring. Eared seals and the Walrus use the foreflippers for swimming.

The eyes of pinnipedes are adapted for underwater vision by virtue of having a flattened cornea, which makes them shortsighted out of water. The pupils are large and there is a tapetum, which aids vision in conditions of low illumination. The vibrissae or whiskers are, however, used for feeling for food in dim light. The pinnipedes avoid the 'bends' when surfacing from a deep dive by exhaling before they dive. As a result the lungs are compressed, the heart slows down to $\frac{1}{15}$th of the normal rate and the blood is shunted mainly to the heart and the brain while the muscles work anaerobically.

Little is known of the life of pinnipedes at sea. It is presumed that they generally disperse, with some individuals travelling well out of the normal range. For example, Grey seal pups tagged on the Farne Islands off the north-east coast of England have been encountered as far away as Iceland and Norway. The Hooded seal migrates away from sea ice but the Bearded seal remains under the ice using breathing holes.

The food of pinnipedes is mainly fishes but also includes molluscs and crustaceans, the latter being particularly important for newly weaned pups. The selection of prey depends on what is available. Thus, when salmon are running seals eat salmon, and as a result they sometimes cause damage to fisheries.

Although they can sleep in water pinnipedes often come ashore to bask. At the breeding season they gather at traditional sites where the females give birth each to a single pup. The females haul out just before the birth which is very rapid. They identify their own pup mainly by smell. The pups are suckled for a short period (3 weeks in the grey seal) putting on weight rapidly, and are then abandoned, but the young walrus is not weaned until the age of 18 months. The pups of most species are born with a white woolly fur, known as a lanugo, which probably serves to absorb heat from the sun in cold weather. The Common or Harbor seal is an exception. Its pup is born with the adult coat and can swim well a few hours after birth. The pups of the Ringed seal are born in a den under snow.

The breeding season varies with the species. In the ringed seal it is from mid-March to mid-April, in the Hooded seal March to May, in the Grey seal September to November, in the Common seal June to July, in the Harp seal March, in the Bearded seal May to June and in the Walrus in May. The cow comes into season shortly after pupping and is mated on land or in the sea. There is a delayed implantation. All seals mature at 3 to 4 years.

The main predator on pinnipedes is man. Killer whales take a few, Polar bears are a danger to Arctic seals especially Ringed seals, and the Walrus occasionally kills smaller pinnipedes.

Seals have always been hunted for their skins, meat and blubber. Today, mainly the pups are hunted for their pelts. As a result of this persecution concern has been felt for the survival of most species of pinnipedes throughout the world. An example is the Grey seal the population of which reached a very low ebb at the beginning of this century but with protection and the evacuation of people from some isolated islands, for example off the west coast of Scotland, numbers have increased enormously. The total population of this species in Europe is 47,000 of which 39,000 live around the British Isles. Most countries have protective legislation for seals with licensing limiting their hunting. Grey and Ringed seals are hunted in the Baltic. The Monk seal is now very rare in the Mediterranean and survives in a few colonies only and even there has taken to caves for protection.

ARCTIC

HARP SEAL

ORDER	Pinnipedia
FAMILY	Phocidae
GENUS	*Pagophilus*
SPECIES	*P. groenlandicus*

Description: deep chest, giving hunchback appearance. Light grey with black on head and black horseshoe-shaped band along flanks and across back. In females the dark areas are paler and may be broken into spots. Pups white.

Length 2m (6ft). Weight 180kg (400lb). Sexes similar.

Range: Arctic Atlantic, including northern coast of Scandinavia and White Sea. Occasional visitor to northern Iceland and British Isles.

BEARDED SEAL

ORDER	Pinnipedia
FAMILY	Phocidae
GENUS	*Erignathus*
SPECIES	*E. barbatus*

Description: profusion of moustachial whiskers which curl when

Harp seal *Pagophilus groenlandicus*
with pup.

Bearded seal *Erignathus barbatus.*

dry. Four teats instead of the usual
two. Grey with brownish tinge on
head and middle of back. Greyish
brown pup. Length 2·3m (7½ft).
Weight 217–272kg (500–600lb).

Range: circumpolar to northern
Iceland and Scandinavia. Stragglers
to Scotland, Norfolk (England) and
Normandy (France).

RINGED SEAL

ORDER	Pinnipedia
FAMILY	Phocidae
GENUS	*Pusa*
SPECIES	*P. hispida*

Description: round head and blunt muzzle. Light grey with black spots, particularly on back where they may run together. Many of the spots are ringed with pale hair. Pups white. Length 1·4m (4ft 10in). Weight 130kg (300lb). Sexes similar.

Range: circumpolar. Arctic coast of Scandinavia. Also in Baltic Sea and Finnish Lakes of Saimaa and Ladoga. Individuals winter northern Iceland; stragglers to Holland, Germany, France and British Isles.

Ringed seal *Pusa hispida*.

HOODED SEAL

ORDER	Pinnipedia
FAMILY	Phocidae
GENUS	*Cystophora*
SPECIES	*C. cristata*

Description: adult male has enlarged nasal cavity forming the 'hood' which, when relaxed, is slack and wrinkled, hanging over mouth. On inflation forms a large football-sized cushion. Grey with irregular black patches. Silvery blue-grey pup known as 'blueback'. Length 3m (9–10ft). Weight 400kg (900lb). Females slightly smaller.

Range: Arctic Atlantic, including Iceland but not Scandinavia. Stragglers to British Isles.

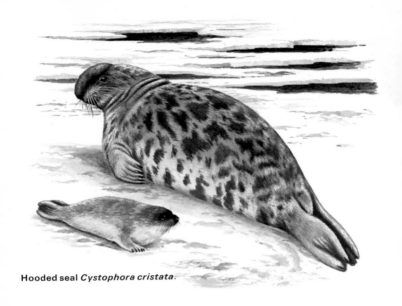

Hooded seal *Cystophora cristata*.

WALRUS

ORDER	Pinnipedia
FAMILY	Odobenidae
GENUS	*Odobenus*
SPECIES	*O. rosmarus*

Description: muzzle blunt with a 'moustache' of stiff bristles and a pair of tusks (the upper incisors) measuring up to 1m (3ft). The hind flippers can be tucked under the body for walking on land. Skin wrinkled, fur short becoming sparse with age. Greyish brown. Maximum length, males 4·3m (16ft), females 2·4m (8ft). Weight (males) 1600kg (3500lb).

Range: Atlantic Arctic.

TEMPERATE

COMMON OR HARBOR SEAL

ORDER	Pinnipedia
FAMILY	Phocidae
GENUS	*Phoca*
SPECIES	*P. vitulina*

Description: dog-like head. Nostrils V-shaped. Colour variable yellow-grey to dark brown with dark spots. Pup as adult. Maximum length, males 2m (6ft), females 1·5m (5ft). Weight 100kg (220lb).

Range: Greenland and Atlantic coast of America south to S. Carolina, Iceland and coast of Europe south to Portugal, Baltic.

Common or Harbor seal *Phoca vitulina*.

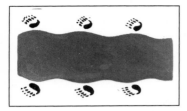

Track left by Common seal moving from right to left.

Food of the Common seal consists mainly of fish, both flatfish (1) and others (2) that are readily available.

Grey or Atlantic seal
Halichoerus grypus.

238

GREY OR ATLANTIC SEAL

ORDER	Pinnipedia
FAMILY	Phocidae
GENUS	*Halichoerus*
SPECIES	*H. grypus*

Description: convex snout, pronounced in adult males which have a 'Roman nose'. Nostrils vertical. Males dark brown or black with pale spots or blotches. Females paler with dark markings. Pups white. Maximum length, males 3·8m (12ft), females 2·4m (7ft). Weight, males 320kg (700lb), females 250kg (550lb).

Range: Atlantic coast of Iceland and coasts of Europe south to English Channel, east to Murmansk.

MEDITERRANEAN

MONK SEAL

ORDER	Pinnipedia
FAMILY	Phocidae
GENUS	*Monachus*
SPECIES	*M. monachus*

Description: chocolate brown on back, greyish underneath, some-

Monk seal
Monachus monachus.

times with white patch. Length 2·7m (9ft), weight 320kg (700lb).

Range: very scattered. Western coast of Africa to Cap Blanc. Desertas Islands. Alhucemas Bay in Morocco, Black Sea. El Arish, Corsica, Salonika, Turkey, Rhodes.

WHALES

The order Cetacea is divided into two suborders: the Odontoceti or toothed whales and the Mystaceti or baleen whales. All are completely marine and breed in water. Their forelimbs ˉare modified to paddles, the hindlimbs are lost. The tail has developed two horizontal flukes for swimming. The nostrils have migrated to the top of the head and form a blowhole, so the front of the head is an enormous upperlip. The streamlined shape of cetaceans is due to an insulation of blubber under the skin. The sense of smell is absent and sight is poor. Hearing is excellent and many, if not all, cetaceans call to each other and may be heard over many miles due to the good conduction of sound through water. Dolphins use echo-location for navigation and food finding. Adaptations for diving are similar to those of seals but cetaceans inhale before a dive and the air in the lungs is pushed into non-absorptive regions such as the bronchi.

Baleen whales are so-called from the plates of baleen or whalebone in their mouths. These are used for straining food from the water. Right whales with very long plates charge through the water with the mouth open, while Rorquals (Blue, Fin, Sei, Humpback and Minke whales) are gulpers, taking mouthfuls of water. The main food is crustaceans, such as *Euphausia, Thysanoessa* and *Meganyctiphanes,* copepods, amphipods, as well as the Sea butterfly *Clione.* Fish and squid are also taken,

especially by the Sei whales but Fin and Blue whales also take these to a lesser extent. Rorquals are migratory. The population of the northern hemisphere winters in the south and goes north for the summer. They often pass close to shores on migration and are generally solitary. The single calf is born in warm, tropical water and is taken north to be weaned in the rich polar waters. The gestation is 10—12 months. Weaning is at 6—7 months. Calving occurs every other year.

Odontocetes include the sperm whales and the many dolphins, with a varying number of teeth in the jaws. They feed on squid and fish and often live in schools. Sperm whales are polygamous. Sperm and Killer whales have a 16-month gestation, lactate for one year and breed once in three years, with shorter periods for dolphins. Dolphins swim very fast, up to 40kmph (25mph) through the use of laminar flow, that is, the skin shape changes to 'iron out' turbulence.

Not much is known about the lives of cetaceans as they can be seen only when they come to the surface. Identification is therefore very difficult. Dolphins are mainly identified by their teeth. The shape of the 'blow' of baleen whales is diagnostic but difficult to see if it is windy. Double blow means a Right whale, a single vertical blow, Rorquals, a blow directed forward indicates a Sperm whale. Points to look for are the colouring, and the shape and

Narwhal *Monodon monoceros*

Beluga or White whale *Delphinapterus leucas*

White-*sided* dolphin *Lageno rhynchus acutus*

White-beaked dolphin *Lagenorhynchus albirostris*

241

**Greenland right whale
or Bowhead**
Balaena mysticetus

Biscayan
or North Atlantic right whale
Eubalaena glacialis.

position of the dorsal fin. For toothed whales, movements are not well known, they do not have such defined migrations as the baleen whales.

Baleen whales and Sperm whales are the traditional quarry of whalers and to a lesser extent so are Pilot whales, Killer whales and dolphins. Right whales are nearly extinct and many Rorquals are now very rare. Concern is expressed for some dolphins, especially in the Mediterranean.

ARCTIC

GREENLAND RIGHT WHALE OR BOWHEAD

ORDER	Cetacea
FAMILY	Balaenidae
GENUS	*Balaena*
SPECIES	*B. mysticetas*

Description: up to 350 baleen plates hanging from arched upper jaw. Dorsal fin and throat pleats absent. Tail stock narrow. Head one third of total body length. Black with white or yellowish patch on chin; tail stock may be grey. Maximum length 18m (60ft), baleen plates 3·0m (10–11ft), maximum 4·5m (15ft).

BISCAYAN OR NORTH ATLANTIC RIGHT WHALE

ORDER	Cetacea
FAMILY	Balaenidae
GENUS	*Eubalaena*
SPECIES	*E. glacialis*

Description: upper jaw less arched and lower jaw deeper than in Greenland right whale, baleen plates shorter and tail stock thicker. Dorsal fin and throat pleats absent. Top of head and back in straight line. Head $\frac{1}{3}$ total length. Patch of rough, thickened skin (the bonnet) on snout. Other similar patches on jaws. Black all over, sometimes irregular light markings underneath. Maximum length 18m (60ft).

NARWHAL

ORDER	Cetacea
FAMILY	Monodontidae
GENUS	*Monodon*
SPECIES	*M. monoceros*

Description: distinguished from all other cetaceans by single, spiral tusk of males, and very rarely of females. Forehead rounded, dorsal fin no more than a 4cm (1–2in) ridge. Greyish, darker on back. Young darker; very old individuals may be almost white. Maximum head and body length 5m (17ft), tusk 2·5m (9ft).

Blue whale
Balaenoptera musculus

Fin whale or Common rorqual
Balaenoptera physalus

Sei whale
Balaenoptera borealis

Minke whale or Lesser rorqual
Balaenoptera acutirostrata

Humpback whale
Megaptera novaeangliae

BELUGA OR WHITE WHALE

ORDER	Cetacea
FAMILY	Monodontidae
GENUS	*Delphinapterus*
SPECIES	*D. lencas*

Description: rounded forehead and slight beak, no dorsal fin. Adults usually white; young grey becoming white at 4 years. Maximum length males, 5·2m (18ft), females 0·3m (1ft) shorter.

TEMPERATE

BLUE WHALE

ORDER	Cetacea
FAMILY	Balaenopteridae
GENUS	*Balaenoptera*
SPECIES	*B. musculus*

Description: 80–100 grooves on throat. Dorsal fin small and placed $\frac{2}{3}$ along length of body. Head flat and less than $\frac{1}{4}$ total length. Dark slate blue except for white undersides of flippers, sometimes with white marbling. Underside of body may appear yellowish. Baleen black. Maximum length 30m (107ft). Weight 132–152 tonnes.

FIN WHALE OR COMMON RORQUAL

ORDER	Cetacea
FAMILY	Balaenopteridae
GENUS	*Balaenoptera*
SPECIES	*B. physalus*

Description: smaller, more slender than Blue whale, with snout pointed and dorsal fin larger. Body grey-black, white underparts including undersides of flippers and flukes, with asymmetric colouring on chin and snout which are white on left-hand side and dark on right. Baleen bluish-grey except for $\frac{1}{3}$ of plates on right-hand side which are white. Maximum length 25m (85ft). Weight 76 tonnes (75 tons).

SEI WHALE

ORDER	Cetacea
FAMILY	Balaenopteridae
GENUS	*Balaenoptera*
SPECIES	*B. borealis*

Description: smaller than Fin whale but forepart of the body stouter; dorsal fin larger and more sickle-shaped. Throat grooves do not extend so far down body. Grey-black, bluish on back and pale patch on chest. Baleen black, and unusually soft. Maximum length 18m (60ft). Weight 61 tonnes (60 tons).

MINKE WHALE OR LESSER RORQUAL

ORDER	Cetacea
FAMILY	Balaenopteridae
GENUS	*Balaenoptera*
SPECIES	*B. acutirostrata*

Description: much smaller than other rorquals but stoutly built. Flippers and dorsal fin large. Blue-grey back, white underneath. White band across flippers. Baleen yellowish-white. Maximum length 9·5m (32ft).

HUMPBACK WHALE

ORDER	Cetacea
FAMILY	Balaenopteridae
GENUS	*Megaptera*
SPECIES	*M. novaeangliae*

Description: heavily built, head $\frac{1}{3}$ total length. 14–20 throat grooves. Short, blunt dorsal fin, flippers $\frac{1}{3}$ of body length. Tubercles on head and flippers. Rear edges of tail flukes serrated. Body black above, white underneath including undersides of flippers and flukes. Baleen greyish-black. Maximum length 14m (46ft).

BOTTLENOSED WHALE

ORDER	Cetacea
FAMILY	Ziphiidae
GENUS	*Hyperoodon*
SPECIES	*H. rostratus*

Description: bulging forehead with a beak. Slender dorsal fin. Teeth absent except in old males which have a single pair. Dark above, white belly. Maximum length 10m (30ft).

BEAKED OR TRUE'S WHALE

ORDER	Cetacea
FAMILY	Ziphiidae
GENUS	*Mesoplodon*
SPECIES	*M. mirus*

Description: Body dark grey on upperside, yellowish purple with black dots on underside. Length 4·8–5·2m (15$\frac{1}{2}$–17ft).

Bottlenosed whale
Hyperoodon rostratus

Cuvier's beaked or
Goose beaked
whale *Ziphius
cavirostris*

Sowerby's
whale
Mesoplodon bidens

True's
beaked
whale
*Mesoplodon
mirus*

247

SOWERBY'S WHALE

ORDER	Cetacea
FAMILY	Ziphiidae
GENUS	*Mesoplodon*
SPECIES	*M. bidens*

Description: slender tapering head with a beak. One pair of teeth occurs lying one third of length of jaw from tip. Dark above, pale underneath. Maximum length 5m (15–16ft).

WHITE-SIDED DOLPHIN

ORDER	Cetacea
FAMILY	Delphinidae
GENUS	*Lagenorhynchus*
SPECIES	*L. acutus*

Description: ill-defined beak, high pointed dorsal fin with concave posterior border. 30–34 pairs of teeth in upper and lower jaws. Dorsal and ventral ridge from dorsal fin and vent. Black with mainly white underside and white to yellow elongated patch on each flank from below dorsal fin to tail flukes. Maximum length 3m (just over 9ft).

WHITE-BEAKED DOLPHIN

ORDER	Cetacea
FAMILY	Delphinidae
GENUS	*Lagenorhynchus*
SPECIES	*L. albirostris*

Description: similar to White-sided dolphin but with grey band along almost whole length of each flank and a white beak. 22–25 pairs of teeth occur in both the upper and lower jaws.

COSMOPOLITAN

SPERM WHALE

ORDER	Cetaecea
FAMILY	Physeteridae
GENUS	*Physeter*
SPECIES	*P. catodon*

Description: huge cylindrical head more than $\frac{1}{3}$ total length, with narrow underslung lower jaws, each bearing 20–30 conical teeth. Dorsal fin replaced by series of low humps. Small flippers. Dark slate-grey shading to white underneath. Maximum length, male 18m (60ft), female 12·5m (40ft). Weight (male) 51 tonnes (50 tons).

Sperm whale *Physeter catodon*

Pygmy sperm whale
Kogia breviceps

Killer
whale
*Orcinus
orca*

False killer
Pseudorca crassidens

249

PYGMY SPERM WHALE

ORDER	Cetacea
FAMILY	Physeteridae
GENUS	*Kogia*
SPECIES	*K. breviceps*

Description: lacks huge head of Sperm whale and lower jaw is broader. Body more like that of a dolphin but with rounded snout. 9–14 pairs of teeth in lower jaw. Black back, grey underneath. Maximum length 4m (13ft). Weight 320kg (700lb).

CUVIER'S BEAKED OR GOOSE-BEAKED WHALE

ORDER	Cetacea
FAMILY	Ziphiidae
GENUS	*Ziphius*
SPECIES	*Z. cavirostris*

Description: low forehead and broad, blunt beak. Low, curved dorsal fin. Males have two teeth at tip of lower jaw. Body dark above and light underneath. Length 8m (25ft).

KILLER WHALE

ORDER	Cetacea
FAMILY	Delphinidae
GENUS	*Orcinus*
SPECIES	*O. orca*

Description: stout bodied with blunt snout. The tall 2m (6ft) fin of adult males is diagnostic. Black with white underside, extending in broad streak on flanks. Also white oval behind eye. Grey crescent behind fin. Maximum length 9·5m (30ft). Weight 850kg (1870lb).

FALSE KILLER

ORDER	Cetacea
FAMILY	Delphinidae
GENUS	*Pseudorca*
SPECIES	*P. crassidens*

Description: small flippers and dorsal fin. Body uniform black. Length, male 6m (18½ft), female 5m (16½ft).

Common porpoise
Phocaena phocaena

Pilot or Caa'ing whale
Globicephala melaena

Risso's
dolphin
Grampus griseus

Bottlenosed
dolphin
*Tursiops
truncatus*

Rough-toothed
dolphin *Steno
bredanensis*

Common
dolphin *Delphinus
delphinus*

Striped dolphin
Stenella coeruleoalba

251

RISSO'S DOLPHIN

ORDER	Cetacea
FAMILY	Delphinidae
GENUS	*Grampus*
SPECIES	*G. griseus*

Description: round forehead and short beak. High recurved dorsal fin halfway along back. 3–7 pairs of teeth in lower jaw. Body grey, lighter underneath. Length 4m (13ft).

PILOT OR CAA'ING WHALE

ORDER	Cetacea
FAMILY	Delphinidae
GENUS	*Globicephala*
SPECIES	*G. melaena*

Description: bulbous forehead, no beak. Slender flippers. Dorsal fin situated halfway along back, very broad at base. Body black with white throat and chest. Length 8·5m (28ft).

COMMON DOLPHIN

ORDER	Cetacea
FAMILY	Delphinidae
GENUS	*Delphinus*
SPECIES	*D. delphis*

Description: slender body with low forehead and long narrow beak. Dorsal fin tapering and recurved. 45 to 50 pairs of teeth in each jaw. Dark brown or black above, white belly with grey, yellow and white undulating stripes on flanks. Black ring occurs around eyes. Maximum length 2·6m (8½ft). Weight 75kg (165lb).

BOTTLENOSED DOLPHIN

ORDER	Cetacea
FAMILY	Delphinidae
GENUS	*Tursiops*
SPECIES	*T. truncatus*

Description: streamlined body with short beak. Lower jaw shorter than upper. 20–26 pairs of teeth in upper and lower jaws. Dorsal fin in middle of back, rear margin strongly concave. Black or dark grey-brown, white belly. Maximum length 3·6m (12ft). Weight 200kg (440lb).

ROUGH-TOOTHED DOLPHIN

ORDER	Cetacea
FAMILY	Delphinidae
GENUS	*Steno*
SPECIES	*S. bredanensis*

Description: little known. Slate-coloured to purplish-black above, with light spots, pale flesh-coloured to white, with grey spots, below. Beak white. 20—27 pairs of teeth in upper and lower jaws. Teeth rough and furrowed. Dorsal fin in middle of back. 2—2·6m (6—8ft) long.

STRIPED DOLPHIN

ORDER	Cetacea
FAMILY	Delphinidae
GENUS	*Stenella*
SPECIES	*S. coeruleoalba*

Description: single immature male 1·35m (4½ft) long, 35·9kg (79lb) weight, stranded on coast of Holland 1967. Very similar to *Delphinus delphis* except in colour; 43 to 50 pairs of teeth in upper and lower jaws. Back dark steel blue. Lighter grey-blue band from top of head to over eye becoming broader and paler as it joins belly. Three bands of ochreous coloration from side of face to along flanks.

COMMON PORPOISE

ORDER	Cetacea
FAMILY	Phocaenidae
GENUS	*Phocoena*
SPECIES	*P. phocoena*

Description: small dolphin with rounded forehead and very short beak. Triangular dorsal fin just behind middle of body. 27 pairs of teeth in upper and lower jaws. Black back and flippers, white belly. Length 2m (6ft). Weight 55kg (120lb).

Index

Page numbers in italics refer to illustrations.